WHAT YOU WAITING FOR, GOD?

Discover the Beauty of Hiddenness

BY SALLY COOK

TRILOGY
PROFESSIONAL PUBLISHING MEETS POWERFUL PROMOTION

olly owned subsidiary of TBN

Waiting For, God?

stian Publishers A Wholly Owned Subsidiary of Trinity Broadcasting

elle Drive Tustin, CA 92780
© 2022 by Sally Cook

Rights Department, 2442 Michelle Drive, Tustin, CA 92780.

Trilogy Christian Publishing/TBN and colophon are trademarks of Trinity Broadcasting Network.

For information about special discounts for bulk purchases, please contact Trilogy Christian Publishing.

Trilogy Disclaimer: The views and content expressed in this book are those of the author and may not necessarily reflect the views and doctrine of Trilogy Christian Publishing or the Trinity Broadcasting Network.
Manufactured in the United States of America
10 9 8 7 6 5 4 3 2 1
Library of Congress Cataloging-in-Publication Data is available.
ISBN: 979-8-88738-105-3
E-ISBN: 979-8-88738-106-0

Dedication

I dedicate this to my amazing family who have journeyed this life with me: Chuck, you inspire me in every way possible and being your wife motivates me to continue growing into the best version of myself; Jill, as my twin, you were God's gift to me in the womb and are the wind beneath my wings; Tom and Ally, your love and truth sharpen me like no one else can; Mum and Dad; you believed in me more than anyone-thank you! And finally, Josiah, I wrote this book when I was pregnant with you and your very presence made me want to follow my dreams, finish this book and not give up on the passion that I have to make a difference in this world.

Endorsements

Sally has been a friend and someone I have enjoyed working with. Her book "What Are You Waiting For, God?" is such a vulnerable picture of her own life experience which she uses to interpret the journey of waiting and hiddenness with a bold lens of love and identity. Talk about life application! If you or any of your friends or family are going through a process that you don't understand in your connection with God, you might just find yourself and your resolution on these pages! I was going to quickly read it and turn in my review, but I found myself praying and seeing different people in my life in various processes of this very journey, knowing that in their reading of this, they have a high likelihood of getting healed from some misunderstandings in their relationship with God. I don't know of any book out in the Christian market that offers so much hope to mature Christians who are questioning their relational process with God.

—Shawn Bolz
Senior pastor of Expression58, author of
Keys to Heaven's Economy and others

Learning to embrace our season of hiddenness is such an important and timely message. I am so thankful that Sally Cook had the courage to go deep into the hard places to find the gold. How many of us have a dream that we are still waiting to see God fulfill? Sally helps us realize that there is beauty in hidden places. It is in the hiddenness where God is forming, shaping, and preparing us to carry what will be birthed. "What Are You Waiting For, God?" will inspire you to embrace all seasons of life, even the ones that don't exactly look like what you had hoped for. This book will help you trust that God's timing is always perfect and that He is working behind the scenes even now on your behalf as you cling to Him in all seasons of life. As you read the beauty of hiddenness, may fire fall upon dormant dreams you once thought dead, and may new hope arise with resurrection power. God sees you and has not forgotten you. He knows what He is doing. You can trust Him and rest in His perfect peace as you wait on Him for promises fulfilled.

—Jennifer A. Miskov, PhD
Author and founding director of
Destiny House Redding

Table of Contents

Foreword...9

Introduction......................................13

Chapter 1: What Is Hiddenness?....................19

Chapter 2: Survive or Thrive 25

Chapter 3: Search for Approval 45

Chapter 4: Son....................................59

Chapter 5: Waiting 77

Chapter 6: Waiting and Waiting and................97

Chapter 7: Transformation 139

Chapter 8: To Be Embraced 151

References..161

To sign up for coaching or to contact the author.

Email: sallycook11@gmail.com

Foreword

My husband Rolland and I have been missionaries for over thirty years as the founding directors of Iris Global. We have bases around the world and over 10,000 churches in Mozambique. Jesus is healing the sick, saving the lost, feeding the hungry, and restoring the brokenhearted. I do not take any credit for what God does through Iris; I am just a little mama in the dirt who yields to Daddy God. What people don't always realize is that Rolland and I spent many years in hiddenness, completely unseen and unknown by anyone except for the poor we were ministering to. During the first ten years in Mozambique, we lived in very challenging conditions praying in our meals and eating whatever came in the cheapest, dented, unlabeled cans and pineapples more often than not. We never aspired to have a great ministry, only to be great lovers of Jesus and gather in His beautiful bride.

One of my life verses is John 15:4 (NIV), "Remain in me, as I also remain in you. No branch can bear fruit by itself; it must remain in the vine. Neither can you bear fruit unless you remain in me." All fruitfulness flows from intimacy with God. God wants us to be so connected to Him and deep in His heart that our desires become His desires. He wants to cut away everything in our hearts that does not line up with His perfect will. When we abide in Him, we become more like Him, transformed by knowing His deep love for us. Sometimes the secret place is a hidden place where it feels like God is the only one who sees us and our dreams. Those seasons can feel exhausting as we wait for what He has promised, or they can be a chance to press into Jesus and choose to trust Him for what we cannot see yet.

Sally Cook is a woman who has chosen to let God refine her in the secret place. I have known Sally for many years and have seen her allow the Lord to prune her heart. She is a woman of faith and character. Sally has walked through long waiting periods trusting God at His Word even when she did not see the fruit. She has experienced crushing disappointments when things that she dreamed for died. Even in the toughest moments of her life, she is a woman who chooses to trust the Lord and lean into His faithfulness. She does not give up or give in. Sally shines for Jesus in such a beautiful way and pours out His compassion, love, joy, and faith to all she encounters.

In her book, *What Are You Waiting For, God?* she vulnerably shares her own testimonies of waiting on God and believing even when she could not understand His ways or His timing. I pray that as you read her testimonies, your faith will grow for your own circumstances and that you will be encouraged to trust God more deeply. Sally also uses biblical heroes to demonstrate what hope looks like and to show that our expectations and reality do not always look the same. Some of our ancestors waited many years and suffered difficult times before seeing their promises fulfilled. God's ways are higher than our ways, and sometimes we do not understand the process. Sally uses the beautiful example of a caterpillar: it fully yields itself to the Lord and dies bit by bit. Life, freedom, beauty, and transformation spring forth only after death and yielding.

I would encourage you to read this book and allow the Lord to prune your heart. Let Him refine your hopes, dreams, and expectations. He is a faithful Father, and He has great plans for your life. Sometimes God's timing is not our timing, but the more time we spend in the secret place, the more we trust Him, and the more we want what He wants and dream the dreams of His heart.

Heidi G. Baker, PhD.

Co-founder and director of Iris Global.

Introduction

How beautiful are the days when creativity flows and the presence of the Lord feels so close and real. Days when the mind wonders off to finer things, places of edification and delight, and where the walls to the heart's enemy seem fortified and strong. Nothing seems to be able to break into war against peace and self-assurance. How great are these days. Not to mention the days where the praise flows off people's tongues, and grace seems to flow like a river towards you as if attracting the right people to you and highlighting your essence of being to those around you. It's a delight to be seen and recognized for your gifts and rewarded for the special traits that only you carry, to be respected for the difference you bring to those around you. How beautiful are these days!

However, what about the days when the wall to the enemy of your heart seems broken, and self-doubt and criticism have set up camp? Days when your mind can't hold off from wandering down destructive rabbit trails only to find yourself at a dead end and wondering how you even got there. These days are so prevalent when you find yourself unseen by those around you and camouflaged into the plain background of the larger world that you never wanted to "be like." Or when, no matter your efforts, you remain unrewarded and speed toward the cliff of rejection at a faster speed than ever.

It's amazing how both ends of the spectrum can occur within our lifetime, if not within every year of our life; times of unmistakable celebration of who you are and times of being invisible to the world around you. For some, if not for most of us, we find ourselves feeling at the opaque end of the scale more often than in or at the limelight end, the end that the world despises and rejects and teaches us to run from. From the moment we can remember, we are encouraged to stand out and are celebrated when we do so, and it doesn't take long to learn that being unnoticed or invisible is not welcomed by the world around us. But what if, maybe, just maybe, this is the way it should be, the way it was designed to be? What if here, in the veiled space, the secret, hidden place, there is a purpose, a time meant for greatness to be cultivated, character to be fashioned, endurance built, and above all, humility crafted?

"Hiddenness" is not normally a word that we celebrate. In fact, what comes to your mind when you ponder the word "hiddenness"? For some, I am sure the child-like game of hide-and-seek comes to mind, where one member of the group purposely conceals themselves and waits anxiously to be found by others. Most have discovered that the better the hiding place, the lonelier the time becomes.

Maybe it's a sense of being invisible in a crowded place, acknowledged by some but not truly seen, not known. Or how about someone's life story that has been beautifully crafted onto the written page, yet the book and its cover are shelved away on aisle seventeen of the local bookstore, far above eye level and completely out of sight yet worthy of being read? For me, it conjures up phrases like "out of sight, out of mind," and honestly, this phrase does not feel good to me.

Hiddenness doesn't tend to conjure up images of life and energy; it makes one think of words like hibernation, invisible, unseen, buried, covert, and obscure.

The Bible, however, is full of stories of godly men and women who spent significant years of their lives off center stage, in obscurity. Joseph, for example, spent most of his years as an unknown slave in a foreign land, not to mention his years in jail, where he was completely forgotten and hidden from the world he would one day rule. There's also Moses, who spent forty years as a shepherd in the middle of nowhere, unrecognized as the great leader God had created him to be. Then there's Paul, who spent fourteen years in Tarsus, where there was no record of any public ministry after a spectacular conversion. Sarah is another case, barren for most of her life, yet received a prophecy that she would one day be the mother of a great and favored nation. Yet it was years before the promise of a child was fulfilled. Hannah was the same; she held the dream in her heart and cried out for a child yet went years with the title of "barren" woman. Even John the Baptist, the promised forerunner to the Messiah, spent his formative years in the desert, out of sight and out of the public eye. Finally, of course, there's Jesus, the God-man who was prophesied about for centuries prior to His birth and who spent thirty years of life off the center stage, out of sight...hidden.

So, what if hiddenness is not as negative as we think? What if we looked at hiddenness in a different light or from another perspective, one that holds the thought that perhaps good comes out of the hidden places and that it's very much a part of God's ordained journey of life?

Let's look at nature, for example: take diamonds, dull pieces of coal that, through heat and pressure, get reshaped into something very different and incredibly beautiful, yet it all happens out of sight and in the dark, buried places in the rocks. Think about the caterpillar that finds itself hidden upside down in a chrysalis jacket, where it slowly transforms into a beautiful butterfly, out of sight of the world around it and with no help from fellow creatures.

I believe that there is a lot more to hiddenness than originally comes to mind; that there is a purpose that makes its very existence in our lives worthwhile. Imagine the difference it would make if our view of "hiddenness" shifted from meaningless to significant. From impossible to challenging and from "to be avoided" to "to be embraced" because maybe, just maybe, God is in this place of obscurity waiting to be discovered and, better still, waiting to uncover us.

Chapter 1: What Is Hiddenness?

No one had ever spoken to me about this term "hiddenness," I had never heard it preached about, and I certainly never pondered it in my heart before the summer of 2008. I had never contemplated why Jesus waited thirty years before stepping out in public ministry; in fact, I think it's safe to say that I was clueless in this regard and have met many people in a similar place of unawareness since then. Hiddenness in itself is nothing new but understanding its part in our life's journey is a concept that is fairly unveiled but desperately needs to be communicated.

I think it would be safe to say that all of us experience hiddenness in various capacities throughout our lives. Hiddenness can appear different to each of us depending on who you are and what your circumstances look like:

For some, it's the promise you have received from God or a prophecy that completely resonates in your spirit and is yet to be fulfilled. Time has gone by, and it still feels far from happening, far from being uncovered! Or maybe it's a prayer for "more," a deep cry of your heart for someone or something to come about in your or others' lives, yet it just seems to go unanswered or at least is not readily apparent.

For some, it's the feeling of invisibility that keeps those around you from recognizing your gifts, strengths, and calling. Even when you feel you are giving your best, you are just left feeling undisclosed, unseen, and even unrewarded... just hidden.

For others, hiddenness seems somewhat forced upon you as a sudden illness or disability has knocked you off the stage of life. The loss of a job, a location move to nowhere, or parenthood with years of self-sacrifice ahead. Whether planned or not, all have the means to completely throw off the balance of it being your time to shine.

Maybe it's a combination of all of the above.

The best way I have been able to describe hiddenness is, "The difference between who I know I am called to be and what I am called to do versus my current reality."

Personally, there have been times when it felt like I am in a holding pattern that prevents me from being released into my fullness, it may not be true, but it's certainly how it has felt at times. It's when my current reality seems so far from what I deeply sense it should be, or at least what the world, the church, and those around me say it should be. In some ways, it has some of the same appearances as the wilderness years, yet it's so different.

Wilderness vs. Hiddenness

The hidden years are not the same as the wilderness experience. It is unlikely that we would ever describe the first thirty years of Jesus' life as a wilderness.

The wilderness or desert experience has more to do with being wooed into intimacy, a season where God allows deep hunger to grow in order to draw our hearts away from things that cannot satisfy us and into His arms of love. The wilderness occurs when we are not ready—when healing and restoration are needed, like when the Israelites were lured into the wilderness to worship God. It was an ordained part of the journey on the way to the promised land, even if it was longer than God had desired. He used the wilderness to draw them into intimacy with Himself and to prepare them for the promised land, but their unwillingness and rebellion kept them there. Joseph is another example of someone who we see being drawn, or in his case, snatched away from the comfort of his home and life. Sold to foreigners, he was taken to a foreign land where God shaped him and pursued him in uncomfortable, if not traumatizing, circumstances. The wilderness can often feel barren and dry circumstantially as God draws the heart to a deeper, more intimate relationship with Him.

Hiddenness, however, is more about God's timing and purpose and the waiting that can entail from this. Hiddenness occurs when we are ready, or at least it feels like we are ready. It's when the time seems right from our perspective.

After Saul died, David went into hiddenness when he had the right to be king of Israel. Everyone wanted him to come to Jerusalem to be crowned king, and he had the legal right to do so, yet God told him to wait and only take Hebron, one-fifth of what was rightfully his. David was ready, even the circumstances seemed ready, yet God had a wait sign held up before him. This is a great example of someone who heard and obeyed, unlike Saul, before him, who lost favor with God when he refused to wait to be crowned king. He saw the waiting as irrelevant and went ahead of God's timing. He ultimately lost favor with God because of his disobedience.

Consider how Jesus may have felt at twenty-eight years old. We will look at this more in detail later on, but it's clear that Jesus was ready, willing, and available. However, God's timing for Jesus to be released into the public eye was not yet. For Jesus, the hidden years were the years when there was no spotlight on him; when there were few signs of the Old Testament prophecies about Him being fulfilled; when Jesus wasn't doing the stuff we read about in the Gospels; the years when He was an ordinary man living a normal life.

The good news is that these years were very much a part of the ordained journey of relationship with God. None of Jesus' life is an accident or a mistake. I have no intention of telling you what the Bible doesn't say about the thirty years Jesus lived before being baptized by John the Baptist. The heart of the following chapters is simply to share perceptions and spiritual revelations as I have pondered the life of Christ before His public ministry and how this timing gives us an insight into the Father's priorities for His Son, Jesus, and, therefore, for us. Hiddenness is not a time of passivity or living merely for the moment of release, but a time of refining our character that we need to fully embrace as well as play an active part in it. I believe that what we do see and read about in the Gospels gives us insight into His relationship with God in those years that we don't see.

What we see in Jesus' three years of ministry is a reflection of what was cultivated and established in His thirty years of anonymity.

Some, if not most, of our greatest learning of what it means to be a child of God happens in the hidden years if we allow it. I say "if" because I believe that, in hiddenness, or what can seem like unnecessary, irrelevant waiting, is when a lot of believers tend to either give up, settle for less, or take matters into their own hands. Believe me, I have been tempted to partake in all of the above during my years of hiddenness and have definitely seen fellow Christians take those roads, none of which lead to anywhere good!

If we were given a glimpse into the heart of the Father and what He did in Jesus during His hidden years, then I think we would be encouraged to stay the course, find hope in those times, and even learn to thrive in our everyday experience of it.

Self Reflection

- What do you perceive to be the difference between the wilderness years and hiddenness?

- What image does hiddenness bring to mind?

- Use images, if it helps, to consider where you feel hidden in your life. How would you describe your hiddenness?

- How does your current reality differ from what you know you are called to be and do? How does that make you feel?

Chapter 2: Survive or Thrive

Thrust into Hiddenness

My journey of recognizing hiddenness began around mid-2008 when I started to question whether or not I was right in my relationship with God, as things were not turning out in life as I had expected.

Up to this point in my journey, I had experienced the opposite of being hidden. Life and success had come easily to me, and I enjoyed new experiences that constantly came my way and favor with authority and with friendships. I became a born-again Christian at the age of twenty-five and threw myself into my local church in North London. I soaked up everything that was being imparted and shared in this lively, charismatic body of Christ and loved it. I got involved as much as possible, and my hunger for God grew and grew. I was blessed and found a lot of favor.

Where the prophetic was released, I would always be highlighted and spoken over. Leaders seemed to recognize what God had created me for, and they would make room for me to practice my gifts whenever possible. I often felt that I always seemed to be in the right place at the right time.

Even when circumstances were more difficult, I could feel God's favor and love. I experienced a wilderness time a few years after being born again, but once I was aware that it was God drawing me into a more intimate relationship, I embraced it and recognized my need to grow and mature. I grew in my ability to hear from the Lord, and my times with God became richer and richer and life-giving.

Spiritually, I was thriving, growing deeper and deeper in intimacy with God, and this was reflected in every area of my life. At work, it was the same; I experienced promotions every year, achieved a national award for excellence in teaching after six years in the classroom, and was working as a consultant for our local education authority by 2002. At this time, I was aware of my calling in the entertainment industry and was beginning to push on doors to test this out. For the following four years, doors of favor flung open before me, and I found myself co-hosting a weekly radio program, presenting on a morning TV show, and had begun to produce a fun children's show. God confirmed time and time again that this was where He was calling me, and I was delighted to step out of everything I knew to follow the call.

It would seem from the outside that my root system was becoming firmly established, deep and sturdy, and possibly unshakeable. At least, that is how it seemed until His hand came and enveloped me, hiding me in a way I had never experienced before.

I remember that, shortly after moving to Los Angeles to pursue my media career in 2007, I attended a prayer meeting where I was given a significant word from someone that would reflect the season I was about to enter. She was a sweet-looking Asian woman, and she came running over to me at the end of the prayer gathering. God had given her a picture for me. She saw me sitting in God's left hand, and very slowly, God began to place His other hand over me so that I was cupped between the hands. She said He was using this season to give me a 360-degree view of what He sees and to not despise it! It seemed such an innocent and comforting word at the time but little did I know that she was lifting the veil for me to see what season I was just about to enter.

Having moved abroad to the entertainment capital of the world, I was now living amongst young, talented individuals who were passionate about God and excelling in their areas of ministry or professions. I no longer stood out in the ways I had done previously, which didn't bother me at first but as the season became more intense, my awareness of this seemed heightened, and comparison kicked in.

My circumstances became more and more challenging and not what I had been expecting. My first job was in Hollywood, and although it was a sought-after position, I was working for just above the minimum wage. I did not have a place to call home, was borrowing a car from friends, and, at one point, found myself sharing a room and sleeping on a blow-up air mattress. I was confused as these were not the circumstances I had expected to find myself in when I was following God's call on my life. To intensify matters, I found that I didn't hear so clearly from God about where I was going, and worst of all, it was a time when I felt that I desperately needed to hear from Him more than ever before. My spiritual hunger increased, but I was no longer satisfied with the corporate church experience. It seemed everyone around me was experiencing God on even deeper levels, yet I had never felt more unheard in the heavens.

I would go to exciting Christian conferences and events only to leave feeling a greater sense of lack than when I arrived—like I had a void that God was not willing to fill. I was also painfully aware of still being single in my thirties at a time when my deepest desire was to be married and have children. I was lonely, confused, and anxious for things to change. I began to ask some deep questions that exposed the insecurity in my relationship with God.

Where was the favor I had been so used to? Why did I sometimes feel like I was invisible to God? Most of all, why did I feel like my God was withholding beautiful gifts from me that would satisfy my hunger?

Maybe I had done something wrong? Was I out of favor with God or man? Was I now in the wrong place at the wrong time?

I desperately searched my heart for anything hidden that could be preventing me from receiving. I rebuked and renounced everything and anything I could think of but to no avail. I came close to leaving Los Angeles to return to the UK on several occasions, feeling emotionally bruised and battered, but by the grace of God, I remained on this part of the journey. The reality was, at a time when I least expected it and a time when I felt ready to shine, I felt hidden, and there seemed very little I could do about it.

So, what was God doing? What was He showing me through this?

Let me walk you through an analogy that I think will give you a visual representation of what could be happening at a time like this.

Weak root system = weak tree!

When the root system of a tree is weak, the tree's survival is in danger. If the weather is good and the elements are kind upon the tree, then maybe it could go unnoticed that what lies below the surface is fragile and unsteady. On the contrary, one could assume the opposite, that the foundation of the tree is strong, sturdy, and unshakeable as it bears fruit. However, what happens when the elements are not so favorable? When the rains don't stop pouring, and the winds are harsh and unwavering? Or when pests multiply and find habitation in the once luscious leaves of the tree? Or when the sun takes its turn between the rains to reveal its dominion, soaring the temperatures way beyond comfortable into unbearable? Only now do we see the strength of the origins beneath.

Where it is unsteady, the tree begins to bow and lean. Where it is shallow, it starts to dry up due to not being able to get enough water or rotting as it drowns in too much. Where the roots are fragile and undeveloped, it now begins to show in the lack of luster in the leaves, stems, and branches, not to mention the lack of fruit. Like all of creation would do at this point, it now survives at all costs, letting go of the parts that are unnecessary and maximizing the limited amount of nutrients to let even the smallest part of the once luscious plant have life. It moves into survival mode, and if that means shriveling up and yielding no fruit so that the core of the plant can maintain health to survive the season, then so be it!

No one in their right mind would choose to spend time or at least long periods of time in survival mode.

This is the mode that makes us feel like we are only just treading water and nothing truly worthwhile is happening, like being on a treadmill where a lot of work is taking place, but you are not going anywhere very fast. It's an awful feeling being in this mode. It crushes the spirit as it questions its purpose, and the soul follows suit by contemplating where it took a wrong turn and how to get back on the right path. Days feel like time-fillers, and if this extends for long periods of time, life can begin to just feel hopeless and meaningless. God can often feel absent and quiet in survival mode, and you can end up feeling small and insignificant.

This is exactly how I felt as I was not prepared for the direction my path would take and the hiddenness I was to encounter in those years. I felt a lot of confusion at this time, questioning the decisions I had made, wondering if I had made a huge mistake, and spent many days fighting hopelessness. Some days, it was a crushing experience, and I was full of anguish as I searched for meaning in it all. I plunged quickly into survival mode!

Our Root System

So why is it that we end up in survival mode when it's the

last place on Earth that we would choose to be? What is it that draws us down this path and keeps us there against our will? For the sake of analogy, let's liken our belief system to a tree's root system. More often than not, when our life's path takes a turn that we were least expecting or we find ourselves in circumstances that were not in our fifteen-year plan, we soon find out the strength of our root system and how firmly established we are in God's love and the truth of who He is. We often forget that there is an enemy to our soul that comes to steal, kill, and destroy. He is out to rob us of peace, joy, or worse yet, our sense of righteousness and right standing with God and His creation. Like the unfavored elements against the tree with the weak root systems, so is the enemy to us where our root system or our thinking, our core beliefs, and our identity are not firmly established in God. If the enemy can get us to think his way, then survival mode is the destination ahead.

No time exposes weakness in our root system more than the hidden seasons of life. In the hidden times, the strength of our identity in God is tested, lies are exposed, and doubts and wrong thinking are brought to the surface. They can no longer hide. It is at this point that so many of us fall into survival mode. The enemy of our soul throws punches we weren't expecting, and our response is to knuckle down, seal the hatches and do whatever we can to survive. We may come out bruised, beaten, and hardened, but we will survive!

Jesus said, "The thief comes only to steal and kill and destroy; I have come that they may have life, and have it to the full" (John 10:10, NIV). When Jesus makes a promise, He also provides the means to bring it about in our lives.

Here lies the challenge for us. Survival mode is not the destination God would choose for us at any point in life. God's desire is for us to live life and live it abundantly, not just in the future but in the here and now, whatever your season, and He paid a high price for us to do this. It's called thriving!

So, how do we thrive in the veiled and hidden places, unshaken by being invisible and undistracted by the bright lights that shine on the lives of others? What is it that keeps us steady in the midst of the shadows and stops us from doubting God's promises, striving to achieve them by ourselves, or, worse still, just giving up?

Look at the trees that Jeremiah refers to:

> They will be like a tree planted by the water that sends out its roots by the stream. It does not fear when heat comes; its leaves are always green. It has no worries in a year of drought and never fails to bear fruit.
>
> **Jeremiah 17:8 (NIV)**

Notice how the trees thrive no matter the elements as the roots run deep into the water. Roots are grown in the dark, hidden places in the soil, out of sight, and invisible from above the ground. They are the first part to be established, and where there is a lack of growth and depth, the harsh seasons are an opportunity for it to push down deeper, grow more root stems, and strengthen it! So, what if God's plan in this hidden season includes purposefully exposing weak roots? God wants to show us where our thinking is wrong, where our belief system is lacking, and where we have our identity in the wrong things. In hiddenness, God wants to fully secure us in our relational identity drawing our roots deeper and deeper into Him. Let's take a closer look at what our relational identity actually is.

Jesus' Relational Identity

We read in Luke 3:23 that Jesus was thirty years old when He began His ministry. It always puzzled me as to why Jesus waited thirty years before stepping out into public ministry. It seems strange that He wasn't in the public eye sooner sharing the good news of the kingdom; after all, He was the Promised One, the Messiah. Wouldn't we in the church think, *What a waste of his gifts*, if we saw a young person with so much potential sitting back and waiting?

Why would the Son of God wait so long to begin His public ministry?

Maybe it comes down to the fact that God's priorities are different than ours, and God's priority for Jesus was bringing Him into the fullness of relationship with Him as a man with God. In fact, this has been His priority for man since the beginning of creation in the Garden of Eden as He walked with them daily. He wanted Adam and Eve to know His love and His ways and then to relate to the world around them from that place. You can hear God's pain when Adam and Eve, after they eat the apple, apologize for hiding. As they tell God that they are naked, God says, "Who told you?" God wanted them to live out of who He said they were, not what the enemy told them they were.

Let's define it this way: our relational identity is who we find ourselves to be in our relationship with God and our relationship with ourselves and with others. Who was Jesus before He began His public ministry at thirty years old? We cannot derive the answer by opening up His physical body to see what is on the inside; this just identifies if He is a human and has human organs. However, if we were to look at who Jesus was by His relationships, then we would get a bigger, more unique picture.

Jesus was the son of Mary, the virgin who conceived Him by

the power of the Holy Spirit. He was the son of Joseph, the carpenter. He had brothers and sisters and lived life in a family. He also grew in relationship with God, who He identified as "Abba, Father." In His humanity, Jesus' relational identity is the sum of His relationship with God, Himself, and those around Him. It was based on the intimacy He developed with God, not on what He did or was about to do. Luke says that "Jesus grew in wisdom and stature, and in favor with God and man" (Luke 2:52, NIV). Just like all mankind, Jesus had to grow into the fullness of these relationships as He grew in maturity and age. It is no different for us as sons and daughters of God the Father.

For thirty years, God the Father cultivated a unique, rich relationship with His Son Jesus, training Him in His ways and works, developing a deep character that would fulfill a destiny, teaching Him how to listen to His voice, how to deal with conflict, how to love others as the Father loves. He was developing a humble yet dynamic personality so He could command ultimate authority in the greatest battle that was yet to come. Relationships are so important to God that He made it a priority for His Son Jesus for thirty years before releasing Him into the public eye.

You can also see this reflected in the three years of His life that we read about in the Gospels. His relationship with

"Abba, Father" was still His priority, and He only did what He saw the Father doing. Everything He did came out of this relationship. Remembering Jesus' humanity is key when looking at His relational identity. Acknowledging the resurrected Christ is vital, but it often comes at the cost of recognizing Jesus, the man who had to grow and develop as we do, in relationship with God, Himself, and others.

Paul commends us to be like Christ,

> In your relationships with one another, have the same mindset as Christ Jesus: Who, being in very nature God, did not consider equality with God something to be used to his own advantage; rather, he made himself nothing by taking the very nature of a servant, being made in human likeness. And being found in appearance as a man, he humbled himself by becoming obedient to death—even death on a cross!
>
> **Philippians 2:5–8 (NIV)**

All the rights Jesus had to be God, He laid down and, in humility, chose to walk fully dependent on the Holy Spirit as a human being. The perfect example of humanity; He grew up just like you and me: as a man learning to relate to God and securing Himself in that relational identity.

Even though Jesus was fully God, He laid it down so that He could demonstrate the way relationship with the Father could be done through every season of life, including the hidden seasons.

Thriving in Relationship with the Father

I often wonder what Jesus was thinking and experiencing at twenty-eight years old. Did He know He had two years before stepping into the public eye? Was He okay with the waiting?

We know that at the age of twelve, He was grasping who He was and what He was doing here on the earth. At twelve years old, Jesus wandered away from the group of Jews that had traveled to Jerusalem for the annual, customary Passover celebration. He didn't return with them, and by the time Mary and Joseph found Him, three days had gone by. Jesus was sitting amongst the teachers, listening and asking questions, amazing the people with His wisdom and understanding. It is incredible to think that it was another eighteen years before Jesus entered the public eye.

I believe that Jesus was a very content man at twenty-eight years old, a diligent carpenter committed to His family, happy to be doing what He was doing. As He never sinned (1 Peter 2:22), He was never anxious or frustrated, and He never lived under the fear that He had missed the boat on His destiny or that He was wasting time (1 John 4:18). I have no doubt those things reared their ugly head as He was tempted in every way (Hebrews 4:15) but never once did He give into them and fall prey to their lies that lead to survival mode.

Some people suggest Jesus was doing miracles and healings before He was baptized in the Jordan, but there is no evidence to support that in the Bible. If anything, it suggests the opposite. For example, when Jesus came into His hometown of Nazareth, He began to teach in the synagogues, and people were absolutely amazed.

> "Where did this man get this wisdom and these miraculous powers?" they asked. "Isn't this the carpenter's son? Isn't his mother's name Mary, and aren't his brothers James, Joseph, Simon and Judas? Aren't all his sisters with us? Where then did this man get all these things?" [Ultimately, the scriptures conclude,] they took offense at him.
>
> **Matthew 13:54–57 (NIV)**

Jesus never stood out as a child! He may have had telling moments like when He was twelve years old in Jerusalem, but if Jesus had been walking in these powers prior to His baptism at thirty years old, then He would have likely received a different response. It would have been more like, "I knew there was something different about Jesus" or, "See, I told you He had special gifts that would one day rise to the surface," or something of that vein. However, it was quite the opposite; they were offended by this once ordinary son of Mary and Joseph, the carpenter, who was now demonstrating incredible wisdom and supernatural gifts. Jesus knew everything He needed was found in God, the Father. He was secure in His relational identity as a child of God. His root system was established and deeply secure. That is, He knew who His heavenly Father was and was comfortable and secure as a Son whether He was in the public eye or not. This, in turn, impacted every relationship in His life.

Relationships are God's number one priority and come before any other priority that you or I may have for our lives. Considering we were created for this, it is surprising how challenging this can be for us. I have found in seasons of hiddenness that it was my relational identity that was put to the test. I soon found out the measure of depth and security I had in my relationship with God.

My Relational Identity Exposed

In my hidden season, my circumstances had left me feeling perplexed and crying out to God, and it was here in this painful place of being hidden under God's hand that I came face-to-face with the holes in my relational identity. Suddenly my root system didn't look so strong; its shallow roots were exposed as it became clear that my identity was not as established in God's love for me as it needed to be.

Questions swirled around my head: Am I the sum of my positive experiences in my life? Am I the sum of my spiritual experiences? Am I the sum of prophetic words spoken over me? Can I only thrive and be at peace when life is good and going my way?

God showed me that I was judging Him and my relationship with Him by my circumstances. When things were good, and I felt God's favor, I felt right with God. I thought it was a direct result of my righteousness. So, the seeming lack of God's favor meant that I was somehow wrong with God or He was angry with me. This led to works or me trying to change my circumstances or even myself, and the enemy had me running around in circles trying to earn something that could never be earned: God's love! This is one of the many lies that God exposed in me during this time.

In hiddenness, God exposes the areas of insecurity that we have in our relationship with Him. Waiting has challenged my relational identity and areas that are not secure in Jesus. Experiencing what felt like spiritual lack brought me to question things, search my heart, and seek the truth in His Word of who God is and who I am. Through this hidden time, my identity was becoming more firmly established in who God is and who He said I am.

Secure in the One

Each of us has our own areas that need shaking or that God will want to expose during the waiting. This is about God securing us in who we are in Him.

God is committed to securing your relational identity in Him no matter the cost. Paul promises us in Romans 8:17 that Jesus' Spirit within us is continually witnessing to us our true relational identity, as a child of God first and foremost, loved and accepted just as we are. Throughout our lives, we internalize so many wrong beliefs about ourselves as well as wrong perceptions of God, but He is committed to freeing us from them and securing us in our adoption. It's not about our commitment but about His.

This is how God moves us from surviving to thriving in hiddenness, drawing the roots of our identity deeper into Him so that we are rooted and established in His love. An identity bound to who God says we are and what He's done for us will ultimately reflect in every area of our lives.

Jesus is our perfect example of thriving in all seasons of His life. He never spent a day doubting if His destiny would be fulfilled or whether the Father really loved Him. He was planted right next to the river, in intimacy with God the Father and rooted in His identity as a beloved Son. Circumstances did not sway Him, and He was at peace with God's timing for Him and what He was to fulfill during His time here on Earth. No day was a time-filler; rather, each day was full of relational security and the joy, peace, and deep sense of self that comes from that.

God's timing may be different for each of us, but His priority for us is the same: relationship! Relationships are so important to God that Jesus spent thirty years developing this with the Father, Himself, and others before being released into the fullness of His calling.

Self Reflection

- Is your relationship with God your number one priority? How do you know? Is this reflected in how you spend your time and money?

- Consider what Jesus might have been doing at twenty-eight years old. Does it surprise you that God the Father waited thirty years before releasing Jesus into the public eye?

- Meditate on this for a while and ask the Holy Spirit to show you what a day in the life of Christ looked like at twenty-eight years old.

- Are you secure in your relational identity?

- Where in your life are you experiencing the hand of God coming over you and covering you? How does it feel?

- God's number one priority for you is a relationship with Him. Do you believe this? Where does this not feel true in your life?

- If this is the case, then how does that change your perspective on the way you prioritize your time and your life? Does it change the way you view your circumstances?

Chapter 3: Search for Approval

I've Finally Made It!

The road was covered with people on both sides of the street, and their voices rang out in unison. Exaltations and heralding are heard for miles around as the people grabbed anything they could find, garments, palm leaves, and other leafy branches to spread on the ground and make a path in the road. The donkey was small, but Jesus sat high as He made His way through the chanting crowds honoring Him with shouts of "Hosanna, blessed is the one who comes in the name of Lord."

No one would question whether this man, Jesus, seated on a donkey, had made an impact on this crowd as He now received glorious recognition for the good He was doing. The crowds talked excitedly about the thousands of people who had been fed with only a few loaves and fishes. The abundant leftover was amazing, and not one man or woman was left with a hungry stomach. The fanfare only intensified as Jesus made His way up the hill towards Jerusalem, the great walled city, which He had approached many times before, unseen and unnoticed. The throngs shared about Lazarus, who Jesus had just raised from the dead. Not just partial death, but three-days-in-the-grave dead! Awe and wonder filled the air, and every man and woman ran to play their part in this time of celebrating the one they recognized as "blessed." The children hustled their way to be close to Jesus and to walk alongside this man who embraced them so freely, wanting a touch just to be close to this special one!

The people's approval of this one they call "Jesus" was obvious, and their admiration was displayed for all to see. They called Him "King," "Messiah," "Chosen One," and "Lord." Such popularity and public appreciation by the masses were hard to come by and usually were saved for the likes of kings and royalty. Many would think, *What a great day this is for Jesus, a day to write home to the family about and to herald as a day to always be remembered.*

Many kings went this way before Jesus and, by means of their title, were greeted with a similar kind of fanfare. But this was different. This was not your typical entrance as it was distinguished by one main factor: the one who was being celebrated. Somehow, Jesus took this day in His stride, not as a day to puff up His chest and say that He had finally made it. He hadn't chosen a chariot or a fine throne carried on the shoulders of strong men. No, He chose to ride on a donkey that had never been ridden before. This entrance was unique yet highly significant.

This wasn't a moment of basking in man's praise and approval but a weighty moment of living out a divine prophecy that was part of a bigger story unfolding. Jesus had no need in His heart for the approval and acclaim of those around Him, let alone the masses. He was, however, fully present in the moment as He followed the Father's voice to carry out this act, finding joy in the people's delight and the generous choices to honor and extol Him so abundantly. Yet, "He knew all people [and understood the superficiality and fickleness of human nature]" (John 2:24, AMP) and how quickly this praise would turn to mocking voices screaming for His death in the days to come. He knew that this was not a place to feed His sense of self nor a time to write home about, but a time for humility and keeping close to God.

Our Longing

How we long for moments like this, when the world around us recognizes us for our accomplishment or contribution, for adoration to flow in our direction and acclaim to ring in our ears. Such tribute is exactly what we would write home about and allow it to play over and over in our minds, somehow feeding our self-worth. If we don't long for others' approval, then we often desire the benefits that come from approval, such as money, status, power, friendship, and favor.

We may dream of occasions like Jesus experienced as He entered Jerusalem, ones that are often reserved for celebrities when they attend award ceremonies in black, stretch limousines welcomed by the hoarding masses screaming their names for a glimpse, touch, or signature. The paparazzi capture it all in photos. The red carpet alone sends a message that is loud and clear. No one needs to tell anyone what it means; honor, celebration, tribute, and acclaim. Only a few special people get to walk it in front of the masses who shout with approval.

But what happens when there is no red carpet, and the work of our hands does not get recognized? Where does that leave us, then?

The Search

The search for significance is a condition that has plagued man since the beginning of time when Adam and Eve experienced a sense of separation from God after "the fall" in the Garden of Eden. God created in us the desire to be accepted and loved, so this sense of separation led to a void in man's experience of the world, and a search for meaning and significance began.

We scan the landscapes of our life for words and gestures of appreciation, for the nods of affirmation that somehow give way to worth and validation. Those few moments of acceptance breathe momentary hope, rekindling our sense of value and worth. The moment is fleeting, although meaningful, and leaves a gaping void, starving for even more. What is it about a word of affirmation from a loved one that stamps our heart with worth? Or the support and validation from a colleague or boss that makes our existence feel like it has purpose and meaning? Why do good grades and red check marks on our work or fancy job titles or promotions reach into our very being to assert that we have value?

Let's face it, we long to receive any indication that we are not wasting the air we breathe and the world has a place for us. We look for confirmation that God created us for a reason and that He is shining down on us with delight and approval. We know deep down that God loves us and approves of us, yet our experience of being hidden contradicts this, blackening it all into the background.

Behind the Search

Very early on in life, we learn that the world is not as safe as we thought; not everyone sees us with value and worth. Many times, it's the opposite. The world treats us harshly, and the hand of evil crushes our sense of worth, sending us messages that we are not wanted or that there is no place for us and that we have little or no value. These lies permeate our thinking until they consume us. Before we know it, our experience once again confirms it with a rejection from a friend or a hurtful word from those from whom we seek affirmation. Worse still, wicked hearts abuse our innocence with physical or sexual abuse, and the trust or the love we seek is not there at all. Absent father or mother, neglect, abandonment, and warped friendships seek to dictate our lack of value by the love and respect that they fail to give to us. The result of it all is a deep wound that is hard to patch and repair. Just when we have a moment to recover, the negative experiences assault our worth again, making our surface wound a gaping hole in need of immediate attention.

So what do we do to fill the void?

Does any of this sound familiar? Maybe if we show those around us that we really do have talent and prove to them that we can succeed, then maybe arms of acceptance will once again embrace us. Or maybe if we hear the words "I love you," we'll feel like we are once again wanted and needed. A new job title, a raise in my salary, a few more friend requests, a great performance review, a friend who missed me, a hug in time of need, the list is endless, and all signs of approval and worth to a hungry and hurting heart. So often, we mistakenly receive these things as a sign of God's approval and love. Be careful where you look for it.

Approval in itself is not wrong, and neither is it wrong for us to desire it, but where we seek that approval is crucial! When we sense deep down that we are special and uniquely made for something that deserves to be celebrated, it is actually a good thing beckoning from a holy place within us. If we look to find this in the wrong place, then we will end up like a wave at sea, tossed to and fro.

Jesus knew that there is only one source of approval and unconditional love that is faithful and unshakeable at all times. He grew in this awareness and relationship from the moment He was born, and on this unshakeable rock, He built His worth and identity.

Where Jesus Found Approval

Jesus spent thirty years in anonymity, and at the beginning of Matthew, we read how that anonymity ended and His ministry began.

> Then Jesus came from Galilee to the Jordan to be baptized by John. But John tried to deter him, saying, "I need to be baptized by you, and do you come to me?" Jesus replied, "Let it be so now; it is proper for us to do this to fulfill all righteousness." Then John consented. As soon as Jesus

WHAT ARE YOU WAITING FOR, GOD?

was baptized, he went up out of the water. At that
moment heaven was opened, and he saw the Spirit of God descending like a dove and alighting on
him. And a voice from heaven said, "This is my
Son, whom I love; with him I am well pleased."

Matthew 3:13–17 (NIV)

The most significant thing about this public moment of
approval is that Jesus hadn't done anything yet! Jesus was
not in the spotlight at this point, He hadn't performed any
miracles, and He hadn't spent years in the synagogues sharing
from the Holy Scriptures. He was hidden for thirty years. At
this point in Jesus' life, His heavenly Father declared how
pleased He was with Him. The Father commended Jesus for
who He was, not what He had done or was about to do. The
Father affirmed who Jesus is, "My beloved Son."

If Jesus needed to be somebody significant in the public's
eye to get the Father's approval, then it is unlikely that He
would have waited thirty years to start His public ministry.
Jesus lived in the knowledge that He didn't need to achieve
and be successful in order to gain the Father's approval and
love. His sense of self was fed by His secure identity as a
"Son."

We need to be careful that we don't fall prey to wrong beliefs,
thinking that our circumstances determine God's approval.

Jesus paid a high price for us to live in the unmerited favor of God all the days of our lives. This is the message of grace.

Even though we hear the words of the Father's approval of His Son for the first time at His baptism, I doubt this would have been the first time Jesus heard those affirmations. The Father's love and joy didn't just flow in the good times but also in the more challenging times, the times when Jesus most needed to hear it.

Jesus ran to this time after time and was often found just retreating on His own, receiving love and a sense of worth from the Father.

Knowing His Acceptance and Approval of Me

One time in my early days of hiddenness, I was really struggling with my circumstances. I was lying in bed feeling very low and trying desperately to run to God in my heart and not away from Him. It was such a raw feeling arising as I contemplated the wonderful things that were happening in the lives of close friends of mine. It was hard not to compare myself. One friend, in particular, was being released in a spectacular way. Her organization was launched into the spotlight with a global impact and included frequent travel to Africa, Europe, and The United States. She had an audience with heads of state, royalty, and governmental bodies wherever she went, and she was a voice for the voiceless women and children. At the height of her release, I had never felt more hidden and insignificant. I was working for a ministry, which God so clearly led me into, but was not at all where I had expected to be in this season. I could not see how this fitted in the big picture of my life, and I struggled with this in my heart. I began to get fearful that I might not ever feel that significant and was frustrated by my seemingly insignificant reality. Others were thriving in their gifts and enjoying the glory and recognition. I began comparing myself to people around me who had a genuine heart for the lost and broken and how it moved them into action with great works or moves of compassion. I, however, was painfully aware that my heart lacked fervency. It wasn't that I didn't have a heart for these things; I did! I really did, but somehow, it didn't compare to those around me. It was an honest reality check on how deep those convictions went and how much I was prepared to act on them. As I did this, I came out lacking!

I lay there feeling vulnerable, tearful, and humbled. I pictured myself in the throne room with the Father, standing there before Him, my head held low, shoulders slumped. I felt weak and shameful, trying to receive God's love but, to be honest, I was far more consumed with myself. I soon drifted off to sleep, and what happened next transformed my experience of this hidden season.

God's Acceptance

It was late into the night when I stirred again, but this time, I knew I was not alone. I sensed a tangible presence in the room, and it was like electricity to my senses. I became alert and aware and pinched myself to see if I was dreaming. An overwhelming sense of peace and love rushed through my body. All at once, I felt completely accepted and fully approved of by God. All of the stuff that I was burdened with disappeared. There was no judgment, no conviction, and no disappointment in what I experienced. Just radical pure love! It felt like a divine embrace or a kiss from heaven, and I was utterly consumed by God's love and acceptance. It was the most thrilling experience! I have no idea how long this experience lasted. I only know in what seemed like one of my lowest, most humbling moments, God's love engulfed me. God accepted me just as I was! God reassured me that I am a beloved daughter of the King regardless of my weaknesses and my circumstance. It triumphed over everything that had gone through my mind and spirit only hours earlier.

I woke up in the morning feeling radically different. Nothing had changed since the night before. My circumstances were exactly the same, but I had changed from within! The love and affirmation I felt that night somehow rooted me more securely in Him, and to this day, I can close my eyes and sense the presence I felt that evening. I would not have been able to experience such a powerful encounter of love and affirmation had I not experienced the pain that arose in this humbling season. Hiddenness was the perfect setting for God to show me how much I allowed the world and my circumstances to define my self-worth.

In hiddenness, I questioned why God, my loving Father, would conceal me like this when I felt so ready to be released. However, God revealed a faulty belief that I needed to be someone to earn His approval. In my zeal for more of God and to be more for God, I ended up striving to change my circumstances instead of finding Him in this place and letting Him lead me from there, even if that meant remaining hidden. God's acceptance in this painful place shifted my focus off myself and my circumstances and back onto Him. I no longer compared myself to others and was at peace about where I was, even when those around me were in the spotlight or receiving acclaim. I was now able to rejoice with them and genuinely celebrate them. Ultimately, I began to embrace my hidden season.

As It Was For Him, So It Is For Us

The Father was committed to securing Jesus' identity and worth in His love as a Son, and it is the same for us. The Father wanted Jesus to always know that He is approved of and has value no matter what life threw at Him. So too, it is for us. This relationship between the Father and Jesus cultivated in His years of anonymity gave Jesus peace to live life in His Father's timing. He had nothing to prove and didn't need to become famous or achieve great things to receive His Father's love and approval. So too, it is for us. Jesus' greatness came out of this place of acceptance and approval, not the other way around. Thirty years of hiddenness did not negatively impact Jesus' sense of worth, nor should it for us!

Self Reflection

- Think back over the last month; when have you felt most validated? What were you doing?

- Where do you place your security: money, success, achievement, status, reputation? Sometimes it helps to identify this by considering which one would hurt the most should you lose it in your life.

- Is your sense of identity and validation coming from God or from success or achievement?

- Consider the baptism of Jesus and the validation from the Father. Have you experienced this fully in your life yet? If not, then take time to ask God the Father for this revelation over you.

- What other Bible characters had seasons of hiddenness before being released into the fullness of their calling?

Chapter 4: Son

A Tale of Two Sons

Two very different sons each built a unique relationship with their father. Both of them grew up in the same household with access to the same provision and care. The servants of the house waited on their needs, and day by day, they learned from the world around them and became men.

James was an inquisitive soul with a sense of adventure. He had so many questions about so many things, and through exploration, he liked to test the boundaries around him. John, the older brother, on the other hand, was dutiful and appreciated and respected the order of the world around him. He was a hard worker and enjoyed putting his hand to the plow and seeing the fruit of his labor.

Neither of the sons, however, was deeply satisfied and happy with life.

James' sense of adventure eventually overtook him, and he plucked up the courage to ask his father for his share of the inheritance so that he could go and find himself in the world beyond their home. He loved his father, and although he respected his work ethic and the life he had built for them, he wanted to do it his own way and have the freedom away from the family to do it. To his surprise, his father granted his request, and he was free to do with it as he wanted. Life was good, and the journey ahead seemed bright and full of opportunity. The travel party was equipped, and off he went on his new journey.

John was horrified to find out that his brother had so blatantly insulted his father by asking for a dead man's purse. How could he be so disrespectful and dishonoring? Their duty was to serve in the father's house, yet James had disowned the family for his own gain by requesting his inheritance now, and it felt so wrong to John. It wasn't really spoken about in the house, or at least John never addressed it with his father. Besides, he knew how his father must be feeling and didn't want to stir the pot. Instead, John made a concerted effort to be more diligent and faithful to his father and show him that, at least, he had one son who was worthy of being called that.

James found plenty to keep his attention on the journey. He made many friends and found that his wealth made him the center of attention, which he loved.

There was plenty of money to go around as his father had been generous to him. Likewise, he showed the same generosity to those around him. He partied and enjoyed female attention, which made him feel important. He pretty much chose his friends and learned how to manipulate people, a gift he would use again and again to get what he wanted. The moment James got bored, he moved on to a new part of the world with different goodies to hold his attention. He hadn't done any work yet or sowed his inheritance into anything worthwhile, but when that time came, he would settle down and make more of himself. In the meantime, there was plenty to go around.

Back at the house, John was surprised to see that time did not heal his father's pain over his younger brother's departure. His father waited at the gate for hours, looking down the long dusty road towards the city, waiting for his brother's return. John had not seen this side of his father before, and it puzzled him that he would be concerned when James, his brother, had shown him such disrespect. It was easy for John to pretend he didn't have a brother anymore. Why concern himself over it? He knew that it was up to him now to make his father happy, work the land well, and show him that one of his sons was loyal and good. He woke up early and spent hours tending the farmland, assessing the books, selectively breeding and raising the livestock, and handling the family finances to ensure a prosperous household for his father. After a long, hard day's work, he would come in for dinner, but by this time, the household was settling down for the night, and he had little time with his father. He took pride in knowing that his father was observing him, taking note of his diligence. Surely his father was delighted in him and soon would communicate this publicly for everyone else to know.

The father encouraged his eldest son to take some time out, to have a break to spend time with the family, but John wanted his father to know he was not like his brother and that he would not rest until all the work was done. This day never came as there was always another field to harvest or livestock to move. It was endless but necessary. It infuriated John that his father kept a daily vigil at the gate waiting for James. He cringed at the sight of him standing there while he worked so hard. A cold, icy chill went down his spine as he thought of his brother living somewhere else, spending his inheritance on worthless things. Foolish man!

John was determined to succeed in what he was doing—to show his father who really mattered and who was worthy of such an inheritance.

Far from home and years later, James' life came to a standstill. In all his pleasure, he never thought the day would come when he would spend the last coins of his inheritance. How on Earth had he spent it all without investing anything along the way? Initially, he wasn't worried as he had made a lot of friends in his travels and blessed so many people by giving them what they wanted. Surely they would repay his generosity so he could survive. He considered his father and his work ethic but let the thoughts pass quickly as a sense of shame arose within him. However, before long, that shame consumed him as he found himself alone and alienated by those who once surrounded him. Now he could see them for what they were, nothing but leeches who were loyal when the going was good but selfish when the well ran dry. James was no longer the life of the party, buying the drinks and flattering people's egos. With no money to pay his traveling party, he sent them on their way and was forced to look for work. At this point, anything would do.

Cleaning pig pens and living in the dirt with them was not what James had ever envisioned for his life. He was so hungry, thirsty, and cold, the chilling weather numbing his sense of feeling as he fumbled through his job. There was little compassion for James once he was out of money, and even the pigs seemed to have no mercy in sharing their food with a stranger. He pondered what life was like at his family home, where there was always more than enough. Even the servants had warm beds to sleep in and plenty of food. Desperation led to a change of heart when James realized his only chance of survival was to head home and find refuge in his father's household. Shame and humiliation overwhelmed him as he pictured himself begging his father for forgiveness.

Maybe his father would have mercy on him and let him live with the servants. There was no way of knowing how he would respond, but one thing he knew for sure was that it was worth a try. Otherwise, it was certain death.

The Surprise

This is the story of "The Prodigal Son." The end of this story is a remarkable one: the younger son returned home, where his father greeted him with an embrace, a gesture of love, and acceptance. The father not only robed the younger son with his cloak, which symbolized this acceptance but also gave him his own ring that sealed him once again with authority as his son returning to his glory. The older brother watched the whole scene with bitter disbelief. He is unable to contain his resentment any longer and protests his father's decision to throw a celebration feast in honor of the "long-lost" son returned!

Both sons were equally shocked by their father's response. His unequivocal forgiveness and extravagant display of love and celebration astonished them both. The father's willingness to give James his inheritance was a complete surprise, as was the father's daily trips to the household gates awaiting his son's return. The younger, returning son was expecting his father to reprimand and discipline him.

His greatest hope was to be a servant in his father's house. The older son must have been expecting their father to reject his younger brother or, at best, make him work his way back into the household earning back what he had so selfishly wasted. Even though both had lived in the same house with their father, neither of them knew him or saw him for who he truly was; abounding in mercy and love, slow to anger, rich in grace and forgiveness. Their father hadn't changed; he had always been this way. In their different ways, both sons looked for approval and acceptance in life in the wrong places, whether from others in the world or on the farm from hard work and achievement. Neither was ever satisfied, and even though it was freely accessible to them, neither received the fullness of their father's love and approval.

The Father

"Sonship" is a central theme of the new covenant. Becoming comfortable with our position as sons and daughters of Father God plays a crucial role in us thriving in life. The hidden times inevitably bring us face-to-face with the mindsets and belief systems that lead us to act more like servants than children of God.

Both sons acted with what is often referred to as an "orphan" or "servant" mindset as opposed to living fully as sons.

Servant mentality is opposite to that of a son or daughter and causes us to forfeit what the Father has freely given us. Servants expect to work for their provision as an employee would work for a paycheck. They don't expect to participate in the inner, intimate chambers of the Father and His family.

Look at the father's response in the story and what Jesus told those around Him about their heavenly Father. He addressed the story to both sinners and Pharisees who had gathered around Him. The sinners would have related to the younger son in Jesus' story, making note that the father held no record of the wrong against the youngest son. Moreover, he embraced his son with love and gave him a cloak, a ring, and a pair of sandals. The cloak was given to special guests as a sign of honor and respect; here, the father communicated his son's full acceptance back into the family. The ring represents his seal of authority as his son, and the sandals were a sign that he was not a servant but a son. Servants did not wear anything on their feet. He gave all of these without finding fault. According to the father in the story, his son's position was not impacted by his recent actions. The father communicated this immediately, not giving his son the opportunity to give the speech he prepared about being a servant.

Jesus also addressed the Pharisees who would have related to the older son in the story. The father's response to the oldest son is simple yet enlightening: "'My son,' the father said, 'you are always with me, and everything I have is yours'" (Luke 15:31, NIV). The oldest son had been working so hard for what was already his as a beloved son, but he was too busy to see it. Working the land was great, but his father wanted it to come from a place of devotion and joy, not a place of duty or performance! By saying that he is always with him, the father communicated that his oldest son had lost sight of the intimate nature of their father-son relationship and was living more like one of the servants who does not always have access to the father.

Hiddenness exposes wrong thinking about Father God. Like a torch turned on in a bat cave, hiddenness drives into the light what lurks in the dark. This is not something to fear but something to be embraced so that any block standing between you and the Father's love can be removed.

Personally, I have related to both sons at different times and see how easy it is to fall into servant thinking even though I am a child of God. God exposed many mindsets that prompted me to strive for His approval and earn His love. That included my long prayer times and reading my Bible, which in itself was great, but I found myself questioning God's favor or acceptance when I would miss those times.

Sons and daughters don't need to earn their position; it's their birthright.

The Father loves us because we are His children and wants us to be free so we can be who He created us to be, which includes failures and successes. In my hidden season, I also became aware that I didn't trust that God's plan for my life was good, so it made me want to run, like the younger son, and do it on my own. Making the choice to remain in Los Angeles in the difficult times was definitely the harder choice for me. It would have been a lot easier to go back to the UK and the comfort of what I knew.

A More Excellent Way

Jesus related to neither brother. He showed that there is a different way, a more excellent way to live as a son. If Jesus had been a third brother in this story, He would have behaved differently than His brothers. He probably would have spent quality time with the father, communing in love and enjoying one another's presence.

Jesus would have inquired about His father's plans for the family and sought to know what was in His father's heart, delighting in the conversation. I can also visualize Him spending quality time with His brothers and demonstrating how to thrive in the father's house and how their unique gifting was needed to expand the family's territory and influence. When the youngest son left with his inheritance, Jesus would have seen the pain in His father's eyes and spent time talking to him about it. He would have made His father's priorities His own and undoubtedly set up a search party to find His brother and bring him home to the father's household, where he belonged. Jesus would never have felt the need to work to gain the father's approval but would have worked because it was His joy to do so. Jesus found His worth as a Son in the Father's presence, where His approval and perfect love cast out all fear. He was loved and accepted for just being a Son, and He knew it.

Receiving the Grace to Thrive

Embracing my hidden season liberated me as I began to see God's hand on it and the purpose for it in my life. It was 2009, which was one of the most difficult years of my life. Even though I welcomed hiddenness and was trying to learn from Jesus' walk, something was missing.

Without a doubt, I had never felt closer to God. I was receiving fresh and inspirational revelation, and God was opening up the platform to preach more on this. God was unfolding truths about sonship to my spirit all year, so I was aware that I was in the right place at the right time. Yet this nagging feeling remained. It wasn't until I was on the airplane home to the UK for Christmas break that I was able to articulate it in my journal. Although I felt more intimate with God than ever before and was beginning to see the wonderful fruit of this in every area of my life, I had never felt more powerless! It was a horrible feeling coming from the very depths of me that I could not hide from or ignore. I knew I was a beloved daughter of God, but my heart did not feel it. Little did I know that God was setting the stage for what was about to happen.

On the first night at home in the UK, I had what I can only describe as a spiritual encounter. A loving presence woke me up and filled the room. Suddenly my spirit was alert, so I sat up to pray. It's hard to describe how I actually saw this, whether it was in my mind's eye or a vision; all I know is that I saw my life through the finished work of the cross, almost like a movie of my life playing through a lens of victory. It all made sense at that moment, and the power of what Jesus did on the cross came alive to me in a whole new way. My whole consciousness was filled with gratitude for what Jesus did through His death and resurrection. Scriptures and songs went flashing through my heart. I heard the words "it is finished" again and again and again!

I woke the next morning a new person. The feeling of powerlessness left and was replaced by this overwhelming gratefulness. I was so incredibly Jesus-conscious. He had done it all, He really had done it all, and I believed it from the core of my being. Grace took on a whole new meaning, and I was reading the Bible with different eyes. Over the next ten days, God gave me an understanding of the vision and what He was doing.

The first thing God showed me was something that Paul talks about in Galatians. I had been mixing two covenants in my life; I had been unknowingly trying to live under both the "new covenant" of grace and the "old covenant," otherwise known as the law. If you, like me, didn't think that was possible, then look at this:

> You foolish Galatians! Who has bewitched you? Before your very eyes Jesus Christ was clearly portrayed as crucified. I would like to learn just one thing from you: Did you receive the Spirit by the works of the law, or by believing what you heard? Are you so foolish? After beginning by means of the Spirit, are you now trying to finish by means of the flesh? Have you experienced so much in vain—if it really was in vain? So again I ask, does God give you his Spirit and work miracles among you by the works of the law, or by your believing what you heard? So also Abraham

"believed God, and it was credited to him as righteousness."

Galatians 3:1–6 (NIV)

Paul rebuked the Galatians for their response to a group of
Jews known as the Judaizers, who taught them that, to be
saved, one must not only believe in Christ but must also obey
the Mosaic Law, the sign of which is circumcision. They
had originally been saved by grace through the teaching of
Paul. In preaching this heresy, the Judaizers also attacked
Paul's apostleship and gospel, resulting in a hindrance to
their obedience to God. They were starting to observe some
parts of the law and even considering a complete acceptance
of the law which was leading them into legalism.

Paul is highlighting that it is possible for God to lead you
into a situation and then for you to take over and start to
operate in your own effort.

It's in the tough times or the trials that what's really going
on in our hearts is exposed! Life's hardships identify which
covenant we're operating under. God revealed that often I
started in grace, being led by the Holy Spirit from a place of
sonship, but I would end up working in my own power under
the influence of a servant mindset. When my circumstances
didn't look how I expected them to, I immediately questioned
myself. Did I hear God correctly? Did I pray enough? Was

there sin in my life causing the undesirable circumstances in which I found myself? For me, what started in grace in my intimate relationship with God ended up in works with me trying to make things happen and earn God's favor.

Every time I inadvertently combined the old and new covenants, I ended up powerless! One example of this was how God was operating in our whole family to address the issue of Freemasonry. Each of us heard from the Lord that there were generational curses that God wanted to free us from, and specifically, He exposed freemasonry, which our family line was steeped in. It was amazing how He spoke to each of us individually and led us to pray in this area for the fullness of His freedom. I witnessed significant changes in some of my family members' longstanding problems being resolved, financial issues ending, and breakthroughs in particular areas of their lives. It was wonderful to see God move over the space of months. I, however, didn't really notice much change in my life. I soon began to question if I had prayed enough or correctly or if I needed to do more or if I had missed something. What began as God leading me by the Spirit was now me trying to work out my freedom and letting my circumstances dictate if God was able or willing to do what He promised. My actions exposed what Paul was saying in Galatians 3, I was taking on the law; if I do the right thing, I will be blessed, and if I don't, I won't. It was no longer acting like a daughter but like a servant. It was so subtle, and most of it was probably subconscious, but it was there all the same!

In His goodness, God showed me why I was powerless. Jesus said, "And no one pours new wine into old wineskins. Otherwise, the wine will burst the skins, and both the wine and the wineskins will be ruined. No, they pour new wine into new wineskins" (Mark 2:22, NIV).

Not only are the wineskins useless, but the wine is also lost. I was neither gaining from grace nor the law! As Paul goes on to say, following the law profits us nothing unless we follow the whole law perfectly, which is impossible. No wonder I was left feeling powerless!

Sonship is our position in God's family bestowed upon us by grace, paid for by the finished work of Jesus, and received when we believe Him and what He has done. My experience of life shifted radically since God gave me that revelation of grace and addressed my servant mindsets one by one. I noticed how I prayed like a beggar trying to twist God's arm to bless me. A son does not beg his Father to bless him. A son knows his Father's deepest desire is to bless His children. A son knows that in difficult circumstances, the Father is right there with him and will walk through it with him. Even now,

God shows me when I fall into the trap of thinking like one of the brothers in the prodigal son story.

Whether in hiddenness or in the public eye, Jesus lived every day to the fullest as He was completely secure as God's Son. The good works He did, originated in this secure place of "sonship." That is also what God wants for us. In hiddenness, I learned to live life fully every day in the "now" moment. When we worry about the future or obsess about the past, we are not able to receive what God has for us in the present moment. To break our addiction to living in the past or future, God lovingly gives us only enough grace for right now, teaching us how to interact with His love and live abundantly where we are.

Self Reflection

- Which son in the "prodigal" parable do you relate to the most? Explain.

- What is your response to the father's statement in Luke 15:31 (NIV), "'My son,' the father said, 'you are always with me, and everything I have is yours."

- What servant mindsets do you recognize in yourself?

- What does it mean to begin in Spirit and end up in the flesh trying to attain the goal in human effort? Galatians 3:1–6.

- How would you define grace?

Chapter 5: Waiting

What Does It Mean to Wait?

I am standing at the light, ready to cross the street, staring at the flashing red light that commands me to stay where I am. The road swells with the life of pedestrians and cars going in different directions, each one on a journey. Lights from other streets flash green, ushering people and cars to move forward, yet, here I am, motionless and paused, aware that everything else is advancing except me. My aim is to get to the other side, but I am held back by the wait sign and the moving obstacles between me and my destination.

Suddenly, I am aware that frustration is rising within me, my body showing visible signs of impatience. My foot starts to vibrate as if to urge the lights to change in my favor and end this delay, which is exactly what this waiting feels like. Who wants to wait when they have somewhere to be? This stagnant, time-wasting moment now feels like a barrier to the progress of my day. Everything around me is moving along nicely, yet I am standing still, arrested by the wait sign. Reaching my destination consumes my thoughts; if only there was freedom to move.

If we are honest, the above scenario accurately describes how we feel when we are forced to wait. Waiting makes us feel stagnant and inactive. Waiting makes us feel impatient at the unnecessary delay, shifting our focus to future happenings rather than the present moment. Waiting fosters a sense of irrelevance in the now, drawing our attention to everything else that is moving forward. Well, at least it does if this is your view of "waiting."

The word "waiting" conjures up all sorts of images, such as standing in the checkout line at the grocery store or for the mailman to deliver the daily post. Maybe it's more hopeful, like waiting for the phone call from a loved one or waiting for a bus, convinced it will come but just not sure when. Maybe it's more fearful, like waiting for test results at the doctor's office or an academic exam board. Whatever the image we have, there is a sense that there is a delay that brings all purposeful activity to a screeching halt. Hiddenness often feels like the red light at the pedestrian crossing, and if we are not careful, our initial feelings of impatience and frustration can lead to disappointment…quickly!

We don't have to see waiting in this way. In fact, our perspective of waiting is critical to thriving in this season of hiddenness, and like anything else, adopting God's perspective of our situation makes a world of difference between tolerating this reality and embracing it.

Active Waiting

What if we saw "waiting" differently? What if we shifted our perspective of waiting from passive, inactive moments in time to an active state of being, a place that is just as relevant as when the light is green, and it's all go?

What if we looked at "waiting" more like a pregnancy? I am currently five months pregnant, so this topic is very much on my mind and one that God is speaking a lot about to me. God seems to enjoy creating and cultivating things in secret places, away from curious onlookers. In pregnancy, there are nine months or so of development and growth taking place before we see the child that the expanding womb promises. Nowadays, we get to see snapshots of the baby's growth through ultrasound technology which captures images at various stages. Before ultrasound was available, everything that took place in the womb was hidden from the world's view.

Whether we see the beauty of creation in a womb or not, it doesn't change the fact that there is an awful lot of activity taking place beneath the surface. A baby grows cell by cell, organ by organ, and system by system, and a mother trusts that her body will bear the fruit of a child. She waits with eager expectation along the journey, trusting that her body knows what to do and when to do it. We even use the active phrase "she is expecting" to describe pregnancy. The woman becomes aware of telltale signs that life is forming within; her belly begins to bulge, she feels discomfort as she makes room for growth, and there is often nausea as the body adjusts its hormones and chemistry to cater to this new life. In this way, the role of the mother is simply to trust that the baby will form as it has been created to do so and to nurture herself as a new life forms. She doesn't dig into her womb to make the heart beat or form the ears. Everything the child needs is in the DNA of its cells and available via the mother's systems.

The role of the expectant woman is to watch what she eats, get plenty of rest, and maintain exercise throughout the pregnancy to avoid sickness and cultivate the best possible environment for this new life. How the woman treats her body at this time has a direct impact on the child she is giving birth to. Bad nutrition means the fetus also has poor nutrition. Our behavior during pregnancy will have a direct impact on the baby's well-being before and after delivery.

Pregnancy is an active, expectant, present moment place of being. It's one of hope and trust, believing that at the right time, the right thing will happen.

Granted, we know that pregnancy can only last up to nine or ten months at the most, and more often than not, in hiddenness, we are waiting for an unknown period of time which can feel like we will be eight months pregnant forever. It's here where the challenge really lies.

Trust

The difference between the two scenarios described above—waiting at the red light and waiting during pregnancy—is the ability to trust the process.

More importantly, it is the ability to trust the timing of it all, believing that God is actively at work on our behalf while we wait. Hiddenness is not a time-filler or a delay but a necessary and significant season.

What's the Purpose?

Isaiah knew how it felt to wait when everything seemed ready to go, like a woman eight months pregnant is eager for the birth but must wait a little longer for the child to develop fully.

Isaiah describes his frustration of waiting, personalizing the prophecy for Israel to his own experience:

> Listen to me, you islands; hear this, you distant
> nations: Before I was born the Lord called me;

from my mother's womb he has spoken my name. He made my mouth like a sharpened sword, in the shadow of his hand he hid me; he made me into a polished arrow and concealed me in his quiver. He said to me, "You are my servant, Israel, in whom I will display my splendor." But I said, "I have labored in vain; I have spent my strength for nothing at all. Yet what is due me is in the Lord's hand, and my reward is with my God."

Isaiah 49:1–4 (NIV)

From birth, Isaiah knew he was part of God's plan, that there was a call upon his life. Similarly, we all have a sense that there must be a purpose for our lives, that God had a plan in mind when He created us, and the more God speaks to us about it, the more sure we become. Next, Isaiah compares himself to a sharpened sword hidden in his master's hand and a polished arrow concealed in the quiver on the back of his master. The words "hidden" and "concealed" in this passage speak volumes. Swords and quivers were designed for action, yet here they remain in a state of waiting. "Sharpened swords" and "polished arrows" were painstakingly made by craftsmen-warriors with great attention to detail and endless hours of effort getting them ready for use.

The arrow, for example, must have perfect shafts to give it

strength and stability. Then the feathers are carefully placed to give the arrow flight. Finally, the arrowhead, which gives the arrow accuracy in flight, is polished to make the surface as smooth as possible. Any error in the process, or faulty work, renders the arrow useless for aimed flight. Isaiah expresses the tension of his feelings, primed and ready, having been through great preparation and character testing, yet he feels held in a waiting period.

At this point in history, Isaiah is speaking to the Israelites, who are now captives in Babylon and exiled from their land. This word would have spoken right into the heart of the exiles who were likely struggling from hopeless despair at their circumstances.

Isaiah describes this time as laboring with no purpose and spending his strength in vain in light of God's purpose for his life to be "a display of his splendor"! It's the cry of "whatever happened to the promises, Lord? Where is the fruit of my life, the evidence of Your favor and love for me?" In this way, Isaiah is an everyman, giving a voice to our own pain when our current reality is a far cry from who we know we are in God and what we are called to do on this earth.

Isaiah knows he is called to display the favor of the Lord. He feels he has worked to position himself for God to do this, and he is fully ready for it. Yet, his reality screams the opposite. Instead, they're all held captive, hidden, laboring for nothing, and not a display of glory in sight!

It would be dismal if Isaiah parked in this place of frustration, but he doesn't. Instead, he moves through it, yielding to God's timing and ways, trusting that God will do what He said He would, knowing his reward is in God's hand alone. The word for reward in Hebrew is *"pe'ullah,"* which means wages. In his humility, he establishes that God will determine what is due to him.

Like Isaiah, waiting in a hidden place can be painful and discouraging. It is good and healthy to express that pain. In fact, denying it doesn't make it go away but acknowledging painful emotions in God's presence is key to finding peace.

Where we go with these emotions after we share them with God is what matters. Do we go down a trail of self-pity towards a cliff of rejection and despair, harden our hearts and blame God? Or do we take our emotions captive, focusing on God as a good Father, and choose to trust Him (like Isaiah did) in the midst of the unknown, unpredictable, and challenging circumstances?

I wonder if Isaiah spent time pondering the faithfulness of God in the past and the journey of the Israelite nation up to this point. Whether he replayed the stories of Abraham,

Isaac, and Jacob and how God had made promises that only His miraculous hand could bring about. Maybe as he considered God's nature and intervention throughout Israelite history, Isaiah was able to come to this place of trust again. Remembering how God had brought justice and reward in the past and for others may have helped him align his emotions with the truth of who God is instead of caving into his emotions.

When we don't trust God through this time, it's easy to take matters into our own hands. Author Alicia Britt Chole says in her book on Jesus' hidden years, page 119:

> In hidden years, when God's timing is not our timing and it's in our power to do something about it, whose timing will you choose? Ultimately, our answer to that question depends on whom we really trust.

> *Anonymous: Jesus' Hidden Years...and Yours-*
>
> **Alicia Britt Chole**

Isaiah was ready and therefore positioned to act on his own will to change his circumstances fulfilling God's call on his life. Or at least he could have attempted and strived to do so. He had the influence to create an uprising, force his voice to be heard in high places, fight against his captors, and plan the escape route for the people in captivity. However, Isaiah knows that God has the bigger picture and is behind Israel's current reality and is using all their circumstances for the greater good. He watched as Israel disobeyed God again and again and found themselves enslaved to another nation by their own choices.

Ultimately, Isaiah chose to humble himself and trust that God was in control even though the circumstances were bleak. He had prophetic words to hold onto that God would deliver His people, and He had a set time to do this.

Isaiah was given God's revelation of the coming Messiah, and interfering in this plan was futile. Like the baby within the womb, no mother would dream of interfering in the process of fetal growth; she simply trusts the process is fully in the Maker's hands.

Even though hiddenness is about waiting, it is an active positioning of the heart to embrace the now and trust God with the future. Without a doubt, tension builds up between the now and the "not yet," and learning to live in balance with that tension is key.

Waiting for My promise

When I was thirty years old, I was mature enough in my relationship with God to hear Him speak about my desire to get married and start a family. I felt I was free to either hear Him say I was meant to be single or that He had a husband for me. Either way, I knew He had a good plan, and I trusted that. If He had singleness for my life, I wanted to embrace it and receive the grace to thrive in it, trusting that He knew what was best for me. At this point, I had been in enough relationships to know that I did not want the wrong one, so it was time to seek God's heart, not mine. I knew God was wanting to speak to me on this issue, and I wanted to humble myself to hear and be alert, so I went on a secret fast until I heard from Him on the subject. I, however, didn't trust my own heart, so I prayed that God would speak to my leaders as well. Marriage and babies were such sensitive subjects that most leaders avoided, at all costs, prophesying about them. So I knew I was going out on a limb by asking God to speak to my leaders about God's will for marriage and family in my life.

It was a month and a half before God spoke to me through three different leaders. The first was a friend who received a picture that was so burning in her heart that she had to tell me. She saw the path of a man cross my path and saw the words "equally yoked," then saw a strong partnership from that point. The second word came from my senior pastor, who saw God's protective armor over me and my heart, and that only one man has the key. He had a warning for me to be aware of counterfeits. Finally, another senior pastor spoke into the waiting that she saw before me as God led me to the man that I would marry. Ultimately, He gave me a clear promise that there was an appointed man for an appointed time and that I was to trust Him. God spoke clearly, so the subject was settled in my heart. Little did I know that fulfillment of this promise was still eight years away and that my next few years would have "wait" signs in all the places I least expected.

In my mind, I was getting on in age when I received the promise, so I thought God and I were on the same page and that I would meet my husband immediately! After the initial exhilaration of my promise wore off, weeks turned into months and months into years. Abraham and Sarah's story was of great encouragement to me at the time on the need to focus on God. "Yet he did not waver through unbelief … being fully persuaded that God had power to do what he had promised" (Romans 4:20–21, NIV).

At times in the journey, I wavered in faith, and the voice of unbelief screamed in my mind. There were times I doubted the promise and would cry out to God, "I thought You made me a promise! Where is my husband? Did I not hear You correctly? Did I make it up?" There were times when I was just plain angry with God and His timing. Confusion, fear, doubt, unbelief. You name it, I felt it.

There were times when I felt deep, unrelenting pain. When

I spent time with loving families, I felt mocked by the lack in this area in my life. Even though I struggled with the unknown and why God's timing was different from mine, He's the one I ran to in my pain. When the waiting became unbearable, and all I wanted was to be out of my current situation, I found that the only place of solace and peace for my soul was in His presence, receiving His love.

In the presence of God's love, I asked Him for signs that I was where I was meant to be. In His mercy, God always responded, and I am so grateful. I would receive a word from a friend or stranger, or I would read something that felt like it was written for me. Or sometimes, it was an overwhelming sense of peace that would calm my emotions until the next time.

Even though God's timing made no sense and I felt so ready to be married, I chose at those times to trust God and remember that I was pregnant with His promise and that it would come to a full term in its own time. It was easy to look at my age and biological clock and question God's timing. I was rapidly progressing through my thirties and related to Sarah's laughter at the promise.

I began to recognize the taunting, mocking voice of the enemy or even my own soul saying I was too old, past my prime, and that it would be impossible biologically to have a family if I didn't act soon. These thoughts engulfed me to the point that resisting the temptation to entertain them became an endurance exercise. There were also times when words from friends and family would end up leaving me feeling even worse than I already had, as they questioned my choices or encouraged me to settle for someone I deep down knew was not for me. Over time, I found the most life-giving thing to do was to only address these thoughts when I was in God's presence, surrounded by His love. If I didn't, they would overtake me, leaving me feeling hopeless and disappointed.

If the overwhelming negative thoughts assaulting me on a regular basis wasn't enough, I had an added distraction of men pursuing me—men who deep down I knew were not right for me—presenting me with the temptation to settle for less than God's best. I had the power by myself to do something about my circumstance and change it by acquiescing to what was in front of me, or I could wait for God's timing which was unknown. I can relate to how Ismael came about, Abraham and Sarah's first son, as they tried to fulfill the promise sooner than God had planned and with their own scheme. The temptation to end my current reality by marrying my boyfriend was almost too great to bear. Deep down in my heart, I knew both he and I would be settling for less than God's best for us.

Choosing to trust God in the midst of overwhelming negative emotions and doubt taught me how to thrive in those years of singleness. More importantly, trusting God enabled me to transition from my previous profession to my calling in Hollywood on the other side of the world, where I eventually met my husband, Chuck.

Waiting prepared me to be a better wife and a humbler companion. I learned that my husband is a gift and not a solution, a reward in God's hands delivered in His timing simply because He loves me. Embracing singleness and waiting for my husband was an active positioning of the heart, a constant yielding of my will to God's will and timing, and definitely not a passive delay in my life.

Releasing Expectations

Waiting was challenging at times, but in it, I learned to let go of expectations and begin to live in expectancy, which is an active, present state of being full of hope. So often, we get tied up with our expectations of how life should play out, which are influenced by our worldview, experience to date, belief system, and the influence of those around us. The problem with expectations is that they have an agenda and set us up for disappointment if our agenda isn't met. It seems like a contradiction, but it is possible to let go of all expectations of yourself, God, and others yet be in a place of full expectancy!

Jesus lived every day full of expectancy and hope, whether He was in hiddenness or in the public eye. His self-esteem and sense of self-worth were found in trusting God's faithfulness at all times.

Living in Expectancy

Jesus always lived in a place of expectancy, keeping the tension between the "now" and the "not yet" in balance. It's how He exists now in His deity, which is why He can never be disappointed with us when we miss the mark with behaviors and attitudes!

Imagine for a moment what Jesus experienced at age twenty-eight before He was baptized with the Holy Spirit. Jesus would have seen the suffering around Him, sickness plaguing those He knew and loved, and at some point, death, even that of His own father, Joseph. Also, He would have been acquainted with the Jewish religious establishment, going to Jerusalem on the annual journey to be a part of the sacrificial festivals. For years, He would have watched the house of God turned into a marketplace where the Jews exploited their own people, exchanging money for animals to offer in the holy place. Further still, He was part of Israel, a chosen nation oppressed by Roman rule. Can you imagine what all this did to Him? What would have been going on in His heart watching these hardships but knowing it wasn't yet His time to act? As Jesus grew in the knowledge of who He was and what He was created to do on Earth, tension was formed.

The Hebrews writer gives us insight into Jesus' response to this tension,

> During the days of Jesus' life on earth, he offered up prayers and petitions with fervent cries and tears to the one who could save him from death, and he was heard because of his reverent submission. Son though he was, he learned obedience from what he suffered.
>
> **Hebrews 5:7–8 (NIV)**

Like Isaiah, Jesus cried out to God with loud cries and petitions throughout the days of His life, yet His cries came with no self-pity or sin. Imagine what Jesus might have prayed for:

"Father, My heart grieves as I see Your people suffer under the weight of the oppression, bound in chains that do not belong to them. I feel how this grieves Your heart! Oh, Father, when can I show them Your goodness? When can I show them that it's not religion You desire, but a heart yielded in love to You? I long to demonstrate Your love in healing their sicknesses and diseases and exposing the plans of Satan in their lives. Oh, Father, how You long to set the captives free! Take this burden from My heart as it is too heavy for Me."

How might Jesus have longed to remind Israel they were God's children? How excited must He have been to tell everyone that He came to fulfill the promise to Abraham that "all nations will be blessed through you" (Galatians 3:8, NIV)? Jesus must have suffered seeing all this, yet knowing He was not ready to do something about it. God heard Jesus' prayers "because of his reverent submission." Jesus trusted the Father's nature; therefore, He could submit to the Father's timing and any "wait sign" that the Father held before Him and find peace there. It was all part of learning to obey His Father's voice. Those thirty years were not a time-filler but a time of growth, preparation, and testing.

What Jesus learned in the hidden season, even when it was painful, set Him up to change the entire universe for all eternity in three short years.

As discussed in earlier chapters, Jesus' identity and sense of being were not tied to future promises. Therefore, He was able to live in the tension of now but "not yet." He had no expectation, which comes with an agenda but was living fully in expectancy. Right here is the balance we need to learn in hiddenness. Living with no expectation of God to unfold His plan in a certain way, no expectations of ourselves or others, yet in a place of expectancy. Expectations attach strings, and those strings are influenced by our culture, our experience, and our beliefs.

Expectancy is free of strings. Expectancy is an active and in-the-present moment, full of hope. Expectations in waiting cause pain when they are not met, but we can cry out to the Father and come to a place of yielded submission, letting go of expectation. Here we find peace and hope in our present circumstances.

If our view of waiting were less like the delay at the red light and more like the timing of pregnancy, we would find it easier to remain in the present moment and live with a deeper sense of fulfillment. We would find it easier to let go of how we think our life should look and trust God and His timing and live actively in a place of expectancy where hope reigns.

Self Reflection

- What are you waiting on God for in your life?

- Does it feel more like standing at a pedestrian crossing: stagnant, inactive, where the future is the main focus? Or like a pregnancy: expectant, hopeful, and present-day-focused?

- Do you ever feel like some days are time-fillers? What can make you feel that way?

- Do you trust God's timing? How do you know?

- How do you respond to the tension of the "now" but "not yet"?

- What does it mean to you to let go of expectation yet live in a state of expectancy?

- How can your emotions serve as a barometer to pinpoint questions/doubts you have about God and His love for you?

Chapter 6: Waiting and Waiting and...

The road is long and narrow, and there is little to speak of on the horizon. It feels as though I have been walking this path forever. Did I take a wrong turn along the way? Worse yet, did I take the wrong path altogether? I glance over my shoulder, considering a retreat; only the path that led me here has disappeared. There is no end in sight and no turning back.

This is not at all how we imagine it would be when the journey begins—when we are full of hope and expectation, full of faith and energy to see God move in our dreams, passions, and promises. Pondering the phrase "He always shows up at the eleventh hour" is laughable as the hands of the clock spun beyond the eleventh hour a long time ago. Disappointment and hopelessness become our companions on a journey we no longer want to take. Every ounce of energy we have clings to a thread of hope that there still may be more for us than this barrenness. Inescapable feelings of insignificance shroud us with a sense of invisibility. "God forgot about me" and "I must have missed it" are our new mantras, consuming what little sense of self we had left, making room for depression. Perplexed, we ponder what on Earth happened along the journey and why unanswered prayers have become our experience. It even seems childish to voice the once believed promises, dreams, and desires as they fade more into the background of wishful thinking as the road continues. Now it is about survival. How do we live in the abundance of life with hopeless despair weighing heavy on our shoulders?

Unfulfilled Promises

I first got pregnant when I was thirty-nine years old. I was in Pemba, Mozambique, when I found out, and we were with our dearest friends, and even my brother and his family were present. Heidi Baker, one of my heroes in the faith, was one of the first to know and pray over my womb. My husband, Chuck, and I were over the moon about it all. What's more, I headed straight to the UK after that trip and told my parents and the rest of the family face the face. It was a dream come true, and there seemed something very prophetic about the timing and setting. Joy filled our hearts, and we delighted in other people's responses to the wonderful news!

At eight weeks, I had my first scan, the scan where parents get to see their baby's heartbeat for the very first time. Unfortunately, we never got to experience the pleasure of that. As the doctor did the ultrasound, he could only find the sac; no embryo had formed. There was no heartbeat! We were taken completely by surprise by the news, and it took a day for it to even sink in. I was mortified!

This is not meant to happen; as a child of God, I knew that this was not my portion, but here I was, faced with an empty womb. In desperate tears, I ran straight to God to seek Him on what was going on. The only thing I found was peace. There were no answers or assurances that the situation would change, just peace. We prayed for a miracle; I even felt a lot of faith for it but deep down sensed that I would never meet this little one on this side of heaven. Ten days later, I had a D&C to remove the still empty embryo from my womb. I grieved deeply for the loss of my unborn baby and also for what seemed like the loss of the promise.

I received the promise of a child only a year earlier. It was early morning when I sensed the presence of the Holy Spirit around me as I awoke from sleep. The hairs on my body were all standing on end, and all my senses became alert.

Suddenly, a scripture just popped into my mind from Hebrews and remained there. I didn't know by heart what this verse was, but I remembered the whole chapter was about faith. I quickly got out my Bible and looked it up, and this is what I read: "And by faith even Sarah, who was past childbearing age, was enabled to bear children because she considered him faithful who had made the promise" (Hebrews 11:11, NIV).

In an instant, I sensed that God was promising me children of my own. I wrote it down in my journal and praised God for what I sensed He was saying. It was such an answer to prayer as only weeks before our honeymoon, Chuck and I had started praying about it. We were older than most first-time parents and knew that conceiving could be a challenge and that a pregnancy could be complicated. We wanted to hear what God had to say and not just presume that we would have our own children, especially as adoption was an option for us. Without a doubt, I knew I had received a promise from God that morning and continued to ponder this promise as time went on, trusting that God had a timing and that it would also involve faith.

Losing my first unborn child was excruciating and tough to understand. I continued to ponder the promise that I was given a year earlier and chose to trust God.

Almost six months later, we were overjoyed to find out that we were pregnant again. This was such a sweet timing of the Lord as it was the day we buried my dad, who had just passed away from cancer. The entire family was present, and it seemed a beautiful gift in the midst of our grief. We rejoiced and praised God for this new life as we celebrated my dad's death and homecoming. Bittersweet!

One week later, I had a miscarriage!

Loss and grief consumed me, and I felt completely robbed

by the enemy. The sorrow I experienced was inconsolable some days, and at times, my anguish turned to anger as I questioned the meaning of it all. The promise that I had received now looked impossible to me, and I was left feeling perplexed and alone in my heartache. What happened to the promise? Maybe it wasn't God promising me a child; maybe it was wishful thinking. What had felt so hopeful was now disappearing on the horizon ahead of me, and it felt out of reach and hopeless.

I struggled with doubt and unbelief as I searched the Scriptures to find any consolation in my pain. It was then that God began to speak to me through Joseph's life and the wilderness journey of the Israelite nation.

Joseph's Hidden Season

Young and hopeful, spirited and foolish were the traits of a youthful man who enjoyed favor in life and at home. The youngest of eleven sons and the product of a loving marriage, Joseph had all the hallmarks of a dreamer who believed he was going somewhere and that the world needed what he had to offer. God gave Joseph dreams that he shared with his family.

> Joseph had a dream, and when he told it to his
> brothers, they hated him all the more. He said to

them, "Listen to this dream I had: We were bind-
ing sheaves of grain out in the field when suddenly my sheaf rose and stood upright, while your
sheaves gathered around mine and bowed down
to it." His brothers said to him, "Do you intend
to reign over us? Will you actually rule us?" And
they hated him all the more because of his dream
and what he had said. Then he had another dream,
and he told it to his brothers. "Listen," he said,
"I had another dream, and this time the sun and
moon and eleven stars were bowing down to me."
When he told his father as well as his brothers, his
father rebuked him and said, "What is this dream
you had? Will your mother and I and your brothers actually come and bow down to the ground
before you?" His brothers were jealous of him,
but his father kept the matter in mind.

Genesis 37:5–11 (NIV)

Joseph's family rejected Joseph and his dreams. Time passed,
but the animosity between Joseph and his brothers festered,
and in a horrific act of jealousy and hatred, they plotted their
brother's murder. Ruben stepped in with an alternative plan
(with the secret intent to return Joseph to his father), so they
stripped him of his coat and threw him into an empty well
while they ate their lunch. In a moment of remorse, they
decided that selling Joseph was better than murder and sold

him to passing Ishmaelite merchants. What a devastating turn of events, being sold twice; first, he was sold by his own brothers and again by the Midianites, who sold him in Egypt to one of Pharaoh's officials, Potiphar.

How quickly Joseph's path had changed from delightful to terrifying!

Joseph's path took a dramatic turn that did not line up with the hopes Joseph had in his heart. Now a slave, a favored slave maybe, but a slave all the same with no rights, no inheritance, nothing to call his own. Joseph worked exclusively to benefit the life and dreams of another, his own dreams long gone, left behind with the family that had rejected him.

> The Lord was with Joseph so that he prospered, and he lived in the house of his Egyptian master. When his master saw that the Lord was with him and that the Lord gave him success in everything he did, Joseph found favor in his eyes and became his attendant. Potiphar put him in charge of his household, and he entrusted to his care everything he owned. From the time he put him in charge of his household and of all that he owned, the Lord blessed the household of the Egyptian because of Joseph. The blessing of the Lord was on everything Potiphar had, both in the house and in the field. So Potiphar left everything he had in

WHAT ARE YOU WAITING FOR, GOD?

Joseph's care; with Joseph in charge, he did not concern himself with anything except the food he ate.

Genesis 39:2–6 (NIV)

Joseph found himself in favor and being blessed, even in his slave position. But once again, things were about to turn on him. Joseph consistently rejected the approaches of his owner's wife, a reality that led him into even deeper darkness. Accused of attempted rape, he was now a prisoner in a dungeon as an innocent man. The prison was a cruel place, riddled with disease and human waste. Few men survived long there, and no doubt Joseph contemplated his death in this hell.

It's easy to miss the depths of what Joseph went through when we know the end of the story, but let's remember that Joseph did not have the benefit of reading the story of his life in black and white. From favored son to slave, he was now locked up, rejected, and alone, in the most dismal of circumstances facing a lifetime of captivity. How often did he struggle in his heart with the tragedy God allowed in his life? How many times did he pray for freedom until he gave up asking? Did he entertain thoughts of revenge for the false accusation? Or did he berate himself for foolishly entering into the presence of Potiphar's wife without taking someone else with him? Did he replay the scene with his brothers over and over again, wishing he had kept his mouth shut? How often did he blame himself for the circumstances in which he found himself, longing for a do-over to make different choices?

We can only imagine the shame and disappointment at his seeming failure to do anything right, let alone the fear and depression at contemplating a life lived in misery. The more time went by, the more his dreams dissolved into faint memories. Add to this a foreboding sense that things may never change, and you have the textbook definition of hopeless despair. The only way to cope with hopeless despair is to deaden the heart and pretend the dreams never existed in the first place. God prospered Joseph despite his circumstances. Joseph was being trained for what was to come, but I doubt he would have felt that at the time. When life hits its low point, it's challenging to see purpose and meaning in the circumstances.

Joseph knew what it meant to wait beyond the eleventh hour. In prison, he interpreted the cupbearer's dream:

> "This is what it means," Joseph said to him. "The three branches are three days. Within three days Pharaoh will lift up your head and restore you to your position, and you will put Pharaoh's cup in his hand, just as you used to do when you were

his cupbearer. But when all goes well with you, remember me and show me kindness; mention me to Pharaoh and get me out of this prison. I was forcibly carried off from the land of the Hebrews, and even here I have done nothing to deserve being put in a dungeon."

Genesis 40:12–15 (NIV)

We would not blame Joseph for harboring a secret hope that one day he would be reunited with his family and the cupbearer was his ticket out. Would this random dream interpretation restore God's promises? However, Joseph's hopes were dashed again when we read that the cupbearer had forgotten him, which meant another two years of prison. To Joseph, it was once again the prospect of a lifetime in captivity. Joseph was thirty years old before he stood before Pharaoh, so he was a slave in a foreign land for thirteen years of his life!

It is easy to be hopeful and patient on the road when the horizon is full of the colors of the sunrise. Here, waiting feels momentary, so we can maintain our pace towards the prize of dreams fulfilled. Like the waiting in pregnancy, parents have foreknowledge that pregnancy is approximately nine months. Delivery is inevitable even if they don't know exactly when. But our greatest challenge comes when the road goes beyond the expected distance. When the horizon of destination seems no closer, and furthermore, its colors begin to fade to a lifeless gray. The road traveled yields painful memories, and it doesn't look like the path is changing ahead. This was Joseph's reality.

No one would blame Joseph for losing hope, given the injustice, years upon years of slavery, and overall lack of fulfillment of his life's purpose. Even though we read that God was with him, his circumstances were far from the dreams or prophetic insights he received as a boy. The longer those dreams were deferred, the easier it was for him to lose hope.

I have no doubt that many more dark emotions plagued Joseph, and he fought for his heart and mind. Maybe there were days when he even lost the fight and gave in to despair. It would be foolish to think that he didn't struggle with his circumstances, experiencing days, weeks, or even months of internal darkness.

Yet something sustained him in these dark and difficult times, preventing him from becoming a bitter and depressed man, angry at God for what was happening to him. I believe that even in the midst of hopeless circumstances, Joseph did not let go of hope.

Hope Deferred

Hope or the lack of it is the factor that determines whether one finds the strength to continue the journey, quit the race, or cave in. Take the relationship between light and darkness. Darkness is merely the absence of light. Likewise, hopelessness is merely the absence of hope. In Proverbs 13:12 (NIV), we read that "hope deferred makes the heart sick, but a longing fulfilled is a tree of life." Hope and hopelessness both have a direct impact on the condition of the heart. When the season of hiddenness extends far beyond the eleventh hour, hope, and therefore our heart, faces its biggest challenge.

When you find yourself waiting far beyond what you imagined and, like Joseph, the circumstances of your life no longer reflect what you had once hoped for, hopelessness can settle in. Maybe your desire is to live in health and vitality, but an illness continues to plague your body despite efforts to be healthy. Perhaps you have a laundry list of unanswered prayers that leave you questioning what you heard in the first place. Maybe your loved one died when you asked God to heal them, or maybe you received a promise from God that is logically impossible in your present circumstances.

Finding hope and not letting the heart get sick with doubt, anger, unbelief, and disappointment is the challenge we face under these circumstances and is what Joseph had to face too. How do we hold onto hope in such adversity? Well, there is another story of a group of people that encountered this challenge that may shed some light as to what to avoid.

Repeating the Journey

The Israelites knew what it meant to wait for a promise. After spending 215 years in captivity in Egypt, God brought them to the desert to worship him at Mount Sinai, where He reminded them of a promised land that was theirs to possess (Exodus 19:4). The difference between this group and Joseph is that the Israelites never made it into their place of promise. They wandered the land for forty years, going around the same mountain again and again. Like Joseph, they faced unexpected obstacles. They, too, probably had a different expectation of how things were going to work out and grew tired and disappointed at not having a place to call their own.

What Kept the Israelites from the Promise?

Interestingly, when the Israelites were at the borders of the promised land looking in, twelve men went in to spy out the land and report back to the group. All but two of them came

WHAT ARE YOU WAITING FOR, GOD?

back with evidence that they would surely fail if they tried
to take the land:

> Then they told him, and said: "We went to the
> land where you sent us. It truly flows with milk
> and honey, and this is its fruit. Nevertheless the
> people who dwell in the land are strong; the cities
> are fortified and very large; moreover we saw the
> descendants of Anak there. The Amalekites dwell
> in the land of the South; the Hittites, the Jeb-
> usites, and the Amorites dwell in the mountains;
> and the Canaanites dwell by the sea and along
> the banks of the Jordan." Then Caleb quieted the
> people before Moses, and said, "Let us go up at
> once and take possession, for we are well able
> to overcome it." But the men who had gone up
> with him said, "We are not able to go up against
> the people, for they are stronger than we." And
> they gave the children of Israel a bad report of the
> land which they had spied out, saying, "The land
> through which we have gone as spies is a land
> that devours its inhabitants, and all the people
> whom we saw in it are men of great stature. There
> we saw the giants (the descendants of Anak came
> from the giants); and we were like grasshoppers
> in our own sight, and so we were in their sight."
>
> **Numbers 13:27–33 (NKJV)**

The Israelites made the fatal mistake of comparing themselves to the giants they saw in the land and comparing their desert tents to the fortified cities. Hebrews says that they did not enter the land because of their unbelief, their lack of faith. Hebrews also tells us that "faith is the substance of things hoped for" (Hebrews 11:1, KJV). Therefore, somewhere along the journey, the Israelites had lost their hope, which was the substance they needed in order to cultivate faith when they needed it at the borders of the promised land. Somewhere they lost sight of God's ability to fulfill a promise, choosing instead to focus on the odds stacked against them. Could this have begun during their years of waiting and hiddenness in Egypt?

The Israelites moaned and complained in response to the circumstances and obstacles they faced. God did incredible miracles on their behalf, expressing that He was with them and for them, yet they moaned and complained at the next challenge they faced, feeling that God forgot and misled them. The reality is that they had a lot to complain about, but this attitude is one of self-focus and pride dictated by circumstances that diminishes hope in what God promised. Nothing separates our hearts from receiving God's love like moaning and complaining.

Throughout their journey in the wilderness, their complaining often angered God. This attitude always had consequences, and it jaded their thinking, blinding them to the repeated divine intervention and the beautiful bigger picture of what God promised to do since the time of Abraham. The devastating result is that their loss of hope over the journey left them in a place of complete unbelief when their moment came to enter their promised land. There was no substance of hope in their hearts which is what they needed for faith to arise at the borders of the promised land. How tragic!

It appears that Joseph resisted this temptation to grumble and complain, and I think the very fact that he was given more and more responsibility and favor shows this. I believe Joseph voiced his disappointment to God in the midst of his pain to God, but he did it by humbly yielding his broken heart to the only one who could comfort him. This enabled him to keep his eyes on the giver of the promise—not just the promise—and maintain focus on the bigger picture.

Our tiny perspective on our current reality is a fraction of God's perspective. Delayed waiting endangers us by losing sight of the bigger picture of God's promise, which is always about His plan, His way, and His timing. Once we become self-focused, then it's easy to complain to God or others about our undesirable circumstances, opening the door to self-pity and overshadowing the bigger picture. Hope cannot thrive with self-pity and defeatism. Then, before you know it, the absence of hope leads to hopelessness and despair.

My Hope Deferred

Losing two unborn children in the light of a promise of being a mother to my own children was incredibly challenging. Grief is a journey, and everyone's process of walking that out is unique, but there are stages that we all face in the process.

The days when I felt confused and angry were the hardest times for me. I found myself questioning God's goodness in the light of my circumstances and arranging my own pity party where I would lie on the bed, cry, and get depressed. Hope seemed to be absent as I contemplated what had been lost and the family that I would never have. Why had God let this happen? Had He abandoned me in my time of need? Why didn't He deliver me from these losses? I was His daughter, after all. As hope was deferred in my heart, I would feel so low and helpless. My heart literally felt sick like the writer of Proverbs warns: "Hope deferred makes the heart sick" (Proverbs 13:12, NIV).

When I let those thoughts take up camp, I would feel such a distance between God and me, like He had deserted me when I needed Him most. I hated those times, they were dark and lonely, and ultimately, they never led anywhere productive or good, never!

I knew that the only way to find healing on this journey was to run to God with my heart raw and vulnerable and focus on His character, not my losses. Even when I was angry, I began to run to God with it and let it all out. I found that in those times, I didn't necessarily get answers, but I found peace and so could feel and receive His love and comfort and hear His guiding voice.

On one occasion, I sensed God asking me, "Do you think that I am okay with miscarriage, Sally? Do you believe that I give with one hand and take with the other?"

I was flawed; I wouldn't say I believed that, but clearly, I had accepted some wrong thinking. I considered how all the women in my family had miscarriages, and so it was kind of accepted that miscarriages went with the territory of having children. Maybe I had accepted in my heart, somewhere deep down and out of sight, that God might be responsible. At that moment, I was overwhelmed with God's heart and goodness and had a deep revelation that this loss grieves God more than it grieves me. Suddenly in that place, my spirit man seemed to rise up like a warrior saying, "If it's not okay with God, then it's not okay with me!"

I then went on a spiritual, emotional, and physical cleansing time. I went to see the naturopath about my body and allergies. I received healing prayers for any grief, and we followed the Spirit to deal with any generational curses that may have had an influence on our losses. It was a gradual daily process that I let Holy Spirit lead, and in the process of focusing on who God is, I found my hope arising for the promise He had given us about having our own children.

I had never really grasped how important hope is, especially in the midst of waiting, in adversity, and in the face of challenging circumstances. The enemy loves to bring about hope deferred as it has the power to literally make our hearts sick and weak. Overcoming the obstacles that diminish hope is crucial on this journey. I found that there are two particular enemies to hope that we need to conquer in order to protect our hearts from hope deferred: entitlement and the test of betrayal.

Entitlement

The definition of entitlement is the fact of having a right to something or the belief that one is inherently deserving of privileges or special treatment.

Addressing any sense of entitlement that we have adopted along the journey is a key to navigating the landmines of long, hard periods of waiting. The problem with entitlement is that it is focused on the "self." It holds fast to our rights, what we feel is owed to us in life, or even what we believe we have earned.

Of all people on Earth who deserved greatness or special privileges, it was Jesus, yet He laid down His deity, His access to His godly rights, as something not to be grasped and humbled Himself (Philippians 2:6). There was no sense of entitlement in His heart even though He had come from the Godhead itself. He chose to live a life led by the Father and Holy Spirit as opposed to a life driven by His rights or even His desires, dreams, and God's promises. Humility and entitlement cannot exist together. We also need to lay down any sense of entitlement that we have picked up along the journey of life.

In my grief and anger, I found myself demanding answers from God. I was shocked that He had let me go through these losses, and I wanted Him to speak to me about it. I was His beloved daughter, after all, and somehow, I felt entitled to His response. Holy Spirit led me to read through Job at this time. I was soon humbled as I came face to face with the truth. Even though I am His beloved daughter who should feel free to ask of her Father, God owes me nothing! He owes me absolutely nothing!

Sometimes as believers, we adopt the view that as a child of God, we have rights and privileges that God, our Father, owes to us. In fact, the reality is we are called to die and declare that it is no longer I who lives but Christ who lives in me, which involves laying down our rights as something not to be grasped and being led by the Spirit into all things. Entitlement leads us to be self-focused and make demands on God as if He owes us something when the truth is God owes us nothing! If we were to receive according to what we have earned, then all of us would be separated from God forever because "there is no one righteous, not even one" (Romans 3:10, NIV). The good news is, despite this, He gave us everything! He made a new covenant with us through the sacrifice of His son, Jesus, because He loves us, not because He owed us anything.

In my dark moments, I had to come to terms with the fact that God gives to me and blesses me because He loves me; He answers my questions and speaks to me because He loves, not because He has to. I was humbled!

Nothing turns our hearts away from God quicker than believing that He owes us something. When we don't receive what we think we should, we conclude that He is withholding from us. This thinking rots the heart. Any sense of self-righteousness, a sense that we have earned from God or deserve His blessings, is exposed in hiddenness. Our right standing with God comes through the finished work on the cross, period. Knowing this is crucial to humbling ourselves and addressing entitlement in our hearts. This is the beauty of grace revealed!

Test of Betrayal

In adversity, there is another heart enemy that we need to address; we have to come to terms with God Himself allowing these things to take place in our life. How often do we find ourselves questioning why God has allowed us to walk into a storm of some sort, a broken relationship, a humiliating experience, a false accusation, or even tragedy?

Imagine for a moment one of Joseph's more difficult days. After the cupbearer raised his hope for reinstatement, Joseph experiences the harsh realization his plea fell on deaf ears. He is lying on a concrete prison bed with maybe some moldy straw for warmth if he's lucky, feeling the weight of despair as he ponders his current reality of captivity and loneliness. His momentary vision of freedom faded to gray as he faced a hopeless future. His mind wanders off to his family, and his heart breaks again as his longing to be with them grows. He remembers the betrayal by his own brothers, recognizing he is here in this den of despair because they sold him to strangers. How could they do that? Quickly, he is consumed with rage wondering why God would allow him to face all this. Where was God when he needed rescuing? Where was God to defend him against Potiphar's wife's false accusations? What did he do wrong that even the cupbearer forgot him? These thoughts devour his peace as God Himself seems to have abandoned him to die in this prison.

We all face times when it feels like God betrayed us and an extended time of hiddenness often brings us to this place. Religious answers are of no comfort in times like these. I, too, struggled with why God had allowed me to lose two unborn babies. There was so much promise around each one, and it was devastating to watch all of it disappear so quickly. I knew God could have prevented it; after all, He is God, and I would find myself tormented by thoughts of God not being my protector or helper. This kind of thinking consumed my peace rapidly, and I found myself putting God on trial in my head: Where were You when I needed You?

Jesus also faced this test. "Why have you forsaken me?" (Matthew 27:46, NIV). He cried out to the Father as He hung on the cross. However, there is a distinct difference between the cry of Jesus and our cry. Jesus is the only man who will ever take on the sins of the world as an innocent man and pay the price for them. He bore the wrath of God once and for all and, by doing so, experienced what in His flesh may have felt like the turning away of the Father. It was very real, excruciatingly real, but in actual reality, it could not be further from the truth. Jesus was quoting from the Messianic Psalm, "My God, my God, why have you forsaken me? Why are you so far from saving me, so far from my cries of anguish?" (Psalm 22:1, NIV).

In His anguish, He was drawing the Jews' attention to who He truly was! It's hard to imagine the intensity of that moment and the pain that Jesus faced, but by embracing it, He conquered it (Colossians 2:14).

Whatever separation from God that Joseph felt, or whatever you or I feel in hiddenness, waiting, and adversity, will always be a feeling and not a truth. What feels true when we are experiencing emotional pain is not necessarily the truth. For example, Joseph no doubt felt at times that he had lost favor with God and that he had been forgotten as his circumstances got worse. However, we know this is not the ultimate truth, even though it may have looked that way. It is far from the truth!

Joseph and the Israelites both faced this "test of betrayal" in the long, dark waiting of hiddenness where they felt God had turned His back on them. Nevertheless, how they responded appears to have had an impact on the outcome of their respective situations. For Joseph, he remained in a place of hope while the Israelites fell into hopelessness. Hope is the substance to which faith anchors itself. God fulfilled Joseph's destiny when his family bowed down to him in the famine. The Israelites came out lacking, so when faith was needed to enter the land promised to them, they wavered in unbelief instead. Amazingly, Joseph held onto hope against all odds and so was able to walk into the promised land when the door eventually opened, Joseph passed the "test of betrayal" in his heart, but the Israelites did not.

This was of great encouragement to me in my grief. Even though it felt like God had turned His back on me or the promise of children, I knew it was not the ultimate truth. Only God's truth would set me free in this. I chose to look at His faithfulness in the past and the truth about His character from the Bible and contemplate that daily, even hourly. It eventually silenced the torment, and I soon found myself in a place where I could receive His love and healing in my heart.

We all face a test of betrayal at some point in our lives. Choosing to believe the truth about who God is and what He says He will do rather than the feelings that arise out of your circumstances is a challenge.

Hope's battleground is where we win or lose.

Hope is not in our promises or dreams but in God Himself. We must come to a place where our hope is found in the Lord alone. Maybe Joseph remembered the story his father told him about Abraham, who believed in God and continued to believe that God would make him a father in spite of his age and wife's barrenness. How do we find hope in the Lord in times of extended, unnecessary delay and adversity?

Hoping in the Lord

Hoping in the Lord is a choice to focus on God and His absolutes rather than the changing nature of your circumstances. Hope isn't automatic by any means. On the contrary, it's something we have to make an effort to maintain. Isaiah challenged the Israelites when they were slaves in Babylon and faced great disappointment with the passing of time. They cry out against God as their hope comes under attack: "Why do you complain, Jacob? Why do you say, Israel, 'My way is hidden from the Lord; my cause is disregarded by my God'?" (Isaiah 40:27, NIV).

They felt rejected and forgotten by God—genuine emotions in extended waiting and hiddenness.

Isaiah wrote this chapter in response to their cries. Look at what he focused on. The entire chapter is a buildup of the incredible nature of God, and Isaiah encouraged them to look at who God is and how nothing can be compared to Him, not even great, wealthy ruling nations like Babylon. He heralded God as the creator of all, and that time does not change God or His commitment to His promises. By getting them to focus on God and His greatness, they took their desperate circumstances to gain peace and hope again. He ended with a truth that I believe Joseph grasped in the midst of his journey of waiting:

> Do you not know? Have you not heard? The Lord is the everlasting God, the Creator of the ends of the earth. He will not grow tired or weary, and His understanding no one can fathom. He gives strength to the weary and increases the power of the weak. Even youths grow tired and weary, and young men stumble and fall; but those who hope in the Lord will renew their strength. They will soar on wings like eagles; they will run and not grow weary, they will walk and not be faint.

> **Isaiah 40:28–31 (NIV)**

There are days in the late stages of waiting where all you can do is metaphorically walk, like in the passage, where each step is a task, but if your hope is in the Lord, you will not become faint and give up. I have absolutely no doubt that Joseph faced many days in captivity like this where it was all he could do to hold on with his fingertips, remembering who the God of his father and Abraham was, which gave him the strength to hope. I also believe there were days when Joseph received such grace and peace in his heart that he soared, like in verse 31, even though nothing had changed in his circumstances.

I would phrase an extension of Isaiah 40 like this: "But those who put their hope in their circumstances, their promises, or their dreams shall not change and renew their strength and power; they will be tossed to and from like waves at sea; they shall lose the power to soar as they focus on themselves, they shall run and grow weary, and they shall walk and faint or completely give up."

My Challenge

Holding onto hope was my challenge in the face of two crushing losses. I had days where my heart was heavy, and as Isaiah refers to it, it felt like all I could do was walk. I learned to focus my heart on God Himself and find a truth about His character that I would ponder over and over. I would cry a lot, but I would not take my eyes off the truth. On these days, God sustained me from sinking into depression and despair. Or, as Isaiah puts it, I didn't faint!

There were other days, however, when I felt the love of God so strongly, I would soar in the reality that my past was not my future and that my hope was in God Himself. Those days became more and more as I held fast to who God was in the midst of my circumstance. I found myself believing again in His promise of children of my own and trusted that He was able to do that.

On the Day of Atonement 2013, I found out that I was pregnant again. God had not forgotten me; I had not been abandoned!

In the waiting, in the face of loss or shattered dreams, God had been building in me a character that produced hope, and this hope did not disappoint (Romans 5:5).

I did experience what may have been the beginning of a miscarriage in week eight, but I was now in a place of sure certainty that this was not God, and I stood in the assurance of faith that I would not lose this child. I had a deep knowing that Satan had not given me this child and so could not take him from me. This scare did indeed pass, and Josiah Eric Cook was born on May 13th, 2014. A hope fulfilled, a tree of life. In fact, we painted the tree of life on his bedroom wall to always remember how important it is to hope in the Lord!

Practicing Hope in the Lord

The key to a right response is taking every thought captive the moment you start feeling disappointment, pain, despair, or the weight of hopelessness pressing in. The battle is won in the mind, regardless of your emotions or your circumstance. Like Paul says:

> The weapons we fight with are not the weapons of the world. On the contrary, they have divine power to demolish strongholds. We demolish arguments and every pretension that sets itself up against the knowledge of God, and we take captive every thought to make it obedient to Christ.

2 Corinthians 10:4–5 (NIV)

Taking captive every thought that goes against God's Word can set you free in your mind. Early on, I couldn't recognize these seemingly insignificant thoughts that destroyed my hope, but with time I learned to spot them from far off.

There were days I woke up feeling the weight of the world against me. I had a sense of dread and foreboding about my future before I even opened my eyes!

Thoughts like, *It's too late for me to live the promises from God*, and *God's forgotten me in this barrenness*. In tiredness, it just felt easier to give in to self-pity and allow the thoughts to race around my mind. However, I learned the hard way that allowing these thoughts to race around unchecked always resulted in hours or days of emotional pain that didn't edify or lead anywhere positive. On one particular morning, I decided I did not want to give the enemy any more of my peace than I had already given him. Immediately I stopped and focused all of my attention on the presence of God. I listened to worship songs that lifted my spirit, and then I asked Holy Spirit to help me focus on truth and who God is. He gave me Psalm 103, which looks at the goodness of God. I meditated on it until I could feel the weight lifting.

Then I identified every negative thought and spoke out loud to each one: "Thought of 'God has forgotten me' I know you are not from God! So I break all agreement with you right now in Jesus' name!" It was empowering to subject my flesh to the truth of God's Word, allowing my spirit to soar. I cried a lot as I felt God's love and empathy surround me, I acknowledged the pain in my heart, but I refused to let self-pity take me captive. Even though I found some peace and my focus shifted to the Lord, I had to do this throughout the day as the same negative thoughts from the morning threatened to rob me of peace and joy. I have learned that if you allow even one negative thought past the barricade of your mind, it brings seven little friends, and it only gets harder to resist. I went to bed that night feeling different. I wasn't rising on wings of eagles, and maybe I wasn't even running, but I had definitely avoided the fainting. I awoke the next morning with my hope in the Lord.

We have a choice where we place our hope in the difficult times of waiting. Yes, it's our choice!

Words of Truth

The following are biblical truths that will be challenged in this extended waiting and hidden season. In this season, God will expose anything in your heart that holds itself up against His absolute truth. I had no idea how many little lies were hiding out in my heart until circumstances squeezed them out of me.

As you contemplate these truths, ask Holy Spirit to reveal to you which truths you do not fully believe. He will likely show you where a lie or erroneous teaching entered your thoughts, knowingly or unknowingly, that is now a block between you and Him.

In your own words, break all agreement with these lies and acknowledge the biblical truths I laid out for you. This process renews your mind transforming you from the inside out! God is good. It's all too easy when we look at the challenges that we and others face to come to the conclusion that God is not good. You will never be able to put your hope in a God that you do not ultimately believe is good. Living with the reality that we cannot explain everything and do not understand why God allows certain things is a necessity in the Christian walk and requires that we trust Him.

We need Holy Spirit to reveal God's goodness to us daily despite what our circumstance tells us.

Mark 10:18 (NASB), "And Jesus said to him, 'Why do you call Me good? No one is good except God alone.'"

Psalm 119:68 (NASB), "You are good and do good; Teach me Your statutes."

Psalm 73:1 (NASB), "Surely God is good to Israel, To those who are pure in heart!"

> How God anointed Jesus of Nazareth with the Holy Spirit and power, and how he went around doing good and healing all who were under the power of the devil, because God was with him.
>
> **Acts 10:38 (NIV)**

Romans 2:4 (NASB), "Or do you think lightly of the riches of His kindness and tolerance and patience, not knowing that the kindness of God leads you to repentance?"

Psalm 145:9 (NASB), "The Lord is good to all, And His mercies are over all His works."

First Chronicles 16:34 (NASB), "O give thanks to the Lord, for He is good; For His loving kindness is everlasting."

Psalm 100:5 (NIV), "For the Lord is good and his love endures forever; his faithfulness continues through all generations."

James 1:17 (NIV), "Every good and perfect gift is from above, coming down from the Father of the heavenly lights, who does not change like shifting shadows."

Psalm 34:8 (NASB), "O taste and see that the Lord is good; How blessed is the man who takes refuge in Him!"

God Is for Me

God is committed to you and your freedom because He loves you! There is nothing you can do to change that. Even when your journey may look like God Himself has turned His back on you, it is simply not true. The truth is God has promised that He will never leave you nor forsake you, and He is committed to working all things for your good.

Philippians 1:6 (ASV), "Being confident of this very thing,

WAITING AND WAITING AND . . .

that he who began a good work in you will perfect it until the day of Christ Jesus."

> And we know [with great confidence] that God [who is deeply concerned about us] causes all things to work together [as a plan] for good for those who love God, to those who are called according to His plan and purpose.
>
> **Romans 8:28 (AMP)**

Romans 8:31 (NIV), "If God is for us, who can be against us?"

Psalm 118:6 (NIV), "The Lord is with me; I will not be afraid. What can mere mortals do to me?"

Psalm 56:9 (NIV), "Then my enemies will turn back when I call for help. By this I will know that God is for me."

God Disciplines the Ones He Loves

God's discipline refines us and molds us to be more Christ-like. Punishment is a penalty for sin or mistakes in the past, but discipline is about God preparing you for your future. God's discipline is not about punishment but about transformation.

Hebrews 12:10 (ESV), "For they disciplined us for a short time as it seemed best to them, but he disciplines us for our good, that we may share his holiness."

Second Corinthians 3:18 (NIV), "And we all, who with unveiled faces contemplate the Lord's glory, are being transformed into his image with ever-increasing glory, which comes from the Lord, who is the Spirit."

> Young man, do not resent it when God chastens and corrects you, for his punishment is proof of his love. Just as a father punishes a son he delights in to make him better, so the Lord corrects you.
>
> **Proverbs 3:11–12 (TLB)**

Proverbs 15:5 (NIV), "A fool spurns a parent's discipline, but whoever heeds correction shows prudence."

First Corinthians 11:32 (NIV), "Nevertheless, when we are judged in this way by the Lord, we are being disciplined so that we will not be finally condemned with the world."

Revelation 3:19 (NIV), "Those whom I love I rebuke and discipline. So be earnest and repent."

God's Grace Is Sufficient

God's strength is made perfect in your weakness. Nowhere in life are we more exposed to our inadequacies, insecurities, and inabilities than when we are helpless to change our circumstances in hiddenness. The truth is, being in a place where we can acknowledge and accept our weaknesses is a good thing.

This is where His grace flows like a river, and more importantly, we are able to receive it. Freedom reigns here!

Paul came to terms with this on his journey when he realized weakness is powerful because God does what we can't.

> But he said to me, "My grace is sufficient for you, for my power is made perfect in weakness." Therefore I will boast all the more gladly about my weaknesses, so that Christ's power may rest on me.
>
> **2 Corinthians 12:9 (NIV)**

John 1:16 (NIV), "Out of his fullness we have all received grace in place of grace already given."

Romans 5:3–4 (NIV), "Not only so, but we also glory in our sufferings, because we know that suffering produces perseverance; perseverance, character; and character, hope."

First Corinthians 15:10 (NASB), "But by the grace of God I

am what I am, and His grace toward me did not prove vain; but I labored even more than all of them, yet not I, but the grace of God with me."

Ephesians 2:8–9 (NASB), "For by grace you have been saved through faith; and that not of yourselves, it is the gift of God; not as a result of works, so that no one may boast."

God Is Trustworthy

If you want things to look how you think they should, then God will definitely seem untrustworthy to you. His ways are not our ways, and His perspective is far greater than ours. He cannot be manipulated or coerced into doing things our way, and no striving on our behalf will change that. Human reasoning and understanding are a fragile and fickle place to stand.

Knowing that we can trust God through anything is like standing on an immovable rock in an earthquake; it anchors our peace in Him.

Second Samuel 7:28 (CEB), "Lord God, you are truly God! Your words are trustworthy, and you have promised this good thing to your servant."

Psalm 9:10 (NIV), "Those who know your name trust in you, for you, Lord, have never forsaken those who seek you."

Psalm 40:4 (NKJV), "Blessed is that man who makes the Lord his trust, And who does not respect the proud, nor such as turn aside to lies."

Psalm 118:8 (NIV), "It is better to take refuge in the Lord than to trust in humans."

Proverbs 3:5 (NIV), "Trust in the Lord with all your heart and lean not on your own understanding."

First Corinthians 13:6–7 (NIV), "Love does not delight in evil but rejoices with the truth. It always protects, always trusts, always hopes, always perseveres."

Finding our hope in the Lord on the long road changes what we see on the horizon. Joseph's life should encourage us that God will come through in His perfect timing and that He has a plan to turn our circumstances to our advantage no matter how the journey unfolds. He has promised us that He will use all things to work for our good.

When Joseph was released from captivity, he had two sons whose names reflected his journey. Joseph named his firstborn Manasseh and said,

"It is because God has made me forget all my trouble and all my father's household." The second son he named Ephraim and said, "It is because God has made me fruitful in the land of my suffering."

Genesis 41:51–52 (NIV)

These names indicate Joseph found freedom from his past and was at peace with it, and had also learned to thrive and be fruitful in his hiddenness. We, too, can become fruitful in the waiting and find peace with our circumstances. It's here that the beauty of transformation happens!

Self Reflection

- Are there promises, hopes, or dreams where you feel hope is deferred?

- What are the defining differences between Joseph receiving his promise and the Israelites forfeiting theirs?

- Why does hope matter?

- Identify areas of your life where there is entitlement. Do you ever feel like you put God on trial in your mind?

- Have you ever felt betrayed by God? What is your response to this?

- Which core truths addressed at the end of this chapter do you struggle with the most?

Chapter 7: Transformation

Finding God and His purpose in the different seasons of our life helps us to embrace them. God is fully invested in our transformation in the hidden seasons. Knowing this enables us to let go of our agenda and live in the present moment, receiving all God has for us in the now rather than focusing on fulfilled promises in the future. Grasping the depths of transformation that God wants to do in our lives in the hidden season allows us to enter into what is happening. Our experience is different if we see this season as:

Hidden, not forgotten
Challenging, not impossible
Present, not future
Significant, not meaningless
To be embraced, not to be avoided
Transformative, not stagnant

Finding His perspective of life in hiddenness allows us to welcome what would otherwise be avoided and shunned. Ultimately, God is committed to transforming us into the likeness of His Son, Jesus, and this is a beautiful process that takes time and involves a lot of change. Change is rarely comfortable, but it is an inevitable part of life. Going into a season of hiddenness is for the mature, not the immature.

Unexpected

About a year into my journey in Los Angeles, I was offered a job with a church ministry. I had recently stepped out fully into the entertainment industry after years of testing the call, and working in full-time ministry was definitely not part of my plan or expectations. Although I felt honored to be asked, I immediately rejected the idea and carried on my merry, little way. However, I found no peace over the following days and could not ignore this deep sense that I had to accept the position. I wrestled deep and hard about taking a step that made no sense to me. I was confused and also disappointed that God had this detour for me, but I eventually found peace as I chose to accept that God's purpose and His perspective were not the same as mine. I accepted the position. Little did I know the level of transformation that was going to take place in this next year of my life as I entered into one of the most challenging years of my life.

I joined the team when it was starting up, and although it was exciting, it came with all the things a new venture comes with; unestablished relationships, no home base, developing vision, low budget, and undefined expectations. A lot of us on the team were in survival mode as we were new to Los Angeles and finding our feet. God positioned me in the center of this, and it was the perfect storm for challenging circumstances. God had me situated to expose my wrong mindsets, unbelief, and any heart issues that He wanted dealt with.

Living and working in Hollywood also comes with the spiritual challenges of striving, idol worship, and selfish ambition, not to mention the celebrity culture that can be incredibly intimidating with its reverence for youth and beauty. I found that God used this difficult time to expose any part of my heart or mind that had partnered with these lies. As I have pointed out earlier, God is committed to us thriving where we are planted and for me, to thrive in Hollywood meant coming in the opposite spirit; humility, being spirit-led, having a healthy fear of the Lord, and walking with a servant's heart. In this job, I came face to face with all the Hollywood issues. For example, my issue with striving meant I struggled in accepting and embracing God's detour into ministry for me as it wasn't in line with my plan, and this led to frustration and anger toward God.

God had some deep work to do in me, and He powerfully used the demanding initial years in Los Angeles, in a job I had least expected to be doing, wrapped in the depths of

WHAT ARE YOU WAITING FOR, GOD?

hiddenness, to encourage me to overcome in all these areas. God was maturing me and bringing about transformation within, the old was dying, and new things were being birthed. Dying to self is rarely comfortable! I was in God's refining fire, and it was painful! However, something beautiful was taking place, and this is the irony about transformation; it most often takes place in challenging circumstances where we are under pressure!

Truth about Transformation

The process of transformation whereby a caterpillar becomes a butterfly illustrates this beautifully. There is an enormous amount of intricate activity involved that can shed some light on the process of transformation in our own lives in this season.

The Shift

According to Dr. Lincoln Brower, author of *Inside the Chrysalis*,

> What is happening inside the chrysalis actually begins inside the caterpillar when it's full grown. There are hormonal changes taking place inside the caterpillar. It loses all interest in feeding, starts

wandering around and then spins a little silk pad. The silk pad is spun on the underside of a leaf, or the underside of a plant, and then the caterpillar turns around and grabs that silk pad with its hind legs which have little hooks on them. Once those hooks are in that little silk pad the caterpillar drops down and begins to change its form. In fact, that's exactly what the word "metamorphosis" means: "changing" its "form."

Even before the chrysalis is formed, work has been done. In fact, it has already shed its skin four or five times by this point and has reached a level of maturity that means it's ready for this next stage. The caterpillar is aware that change is coming and moves away from its normal activity; the old no longer satisfies and so finds itself somewhere out of sight, hidden under the leaf in a newly formed chrysalis, ready for what comes next.

The Death

As the caterpillar hangs in the chrysalis, a biological miracle begins to take place. Enzymes are now being released. That digest all the caterpillar tissue so that the caterpillar is being converted into a rich culture medium.

What used to digest the leaf now digests the caterpillar itself.

It literally consumes itself from the inside out, and within this rich culture medium, several sets of little cells called "imaginal disks" are activated. These little groups of cells started developing very early in the caterpillar's life but then stalled and have been in waiting until this point in the transformation process.

It's fascinating how in this medium of death, these previously stagnant cells begin to come alive and activate. These "imaginal discs" are like little groups of embryonic cells. As soon as the metamorphosis gets going in the chrysalis, these little cells start growing like crazy. One imaginal disk will become a wing, another an antenna, another a leg, and this continues for all the organs of the butterfly until it is totally rebuilt.

Finding ourselves in hiddenness often feels like this dying process. It certainly felt like that for me in my initial years in Los Angeles. I had to die to my ways, my expectations of how things should work out, and let go of any control I thought I had on bringing about my destiny. I had to make the intentional choice in difficult times to submit to Christ's lordship in every area of my life. In this time of seeming "death of the old" and intense life change, God was creating a rich medium culture like in the chrysalis, where the beauty of my true self, my true spirit man, and relationship with God was being discovered and coming alive. It's the inner man that has always been there but for some time has laid stagnant, dreams that have laid dormant and undiscovered began to thrive in this environment. What was old and restricting was being put to death while new things blossomed. God was creating space for humility to come alive in me, new levels of faith in love to arise, and a broader vision for my life that was greater than just myself. My perspective was expanding from being all about me to embracing the causes of humanity around me. I also began to understand the depths of being Spirit-led as journeying with God often doesn't make sense. Learning what it means to follow the Spirit is key in this season. It also allowed me to rest from striving as I came to terms with God being the vine and the vinedresser. I learned the lesson that He would fulfill His promises in His timing, and my part is to stay close and believe Him!

Jesus never resisted the work of the Father in His life, and being out of sight and hidden for thirty years created the perfect setting for maturing and transformational living in the present moment.

New Life

> If you were to weigh a chrysalis 3 days after it
> formed, and then weigh the adult about 24 hours
> after it emerges, it would have lost nearly half its

weight. This shows that the process of metamorphosis consumes a tremendous amount of energy.

The beauty of this transformation is that it happens with little help from the caterpillar itself. It shows up and enters into the process, and the rest is established in the nature of its being. Caterpillars were designed to become butterflies; their DNA is programmed to complete this metamorphosis, even though it is painful and intense.

The depths of what God is doing as He takes us through the process of discovering who we are as a "new creation" takes a large amount of energy. As we have seen through the previous chapters, dealing with our false expectations, choosing to trust God, and holding fast to hope are all choices that consume energy. A lot of grace and patience are needed for ourselves in this process. It's like James says: "But let patience have its perfect work, that you may be perfect and complete, lacking nothing" (James 1:4, NKJV).

For the caterpillar to change into the butterfly, it remains hidden. It would be easy to mistake the chrysalis for something that is dead, ugly, and worthless when we don't see anything happening on the outside. In our hiddenness, it may seem an insignificant time, with little taking place and not much movement, but this is a far cry from what is really happening within us.

Paul talks about transformation:

> Do not conform to the pattern of this world, but be
> transformed by the renewing of your mind. Then
> you will be able to test and approve what God's
> will is—his good, pleasing and perfect will.
>
> **Romans 12:2 (NIV)**

As we allow God to transform us in the hidden place, we will begin to see His perfect will for our lives unfold. As the caterpillar transforms into a butterfly and begins to fly, it sees the world completely differently compared to its old original state as a caterpillar, and so it is with us. Our growing maturity will enable us to mature our perspective on our lives and God's work around us. We are far more able to discern between what God's doing in our lives and what He is not doing, what to embrace, and what to reject. For example, following my time working with the ministry in Los Angeles, I was offered two jobs at two different organizations: one was a more prestigious position and would mean global travel, and the other was more challenging and financially less rewarding. Honestly, I was very attracted to the more prestigious position; however, as a result of what God had done in my heart over the previous year, I was now more submitted to Holy Spirit's guidance. I sought counsel and listened for the small voice throughout. I ended up taking the more challenging role. Praise God as this led me right down the same path as the man who is now my husband. Even though I didn't fully understand why this role was opening up, it became clear as I stepped out. The work of patience during the hidden season was doing a great job on my heart, in particular with the issue of striving. I now felt less driven by my ambitions and more led by the Spirit.

Becoming a Christian may set you free spiritually, but you can still live bound up, in control, and not by the Spirit.

"It is for freedom that Christ has set us free. Stand firm, then, and do not let yourselves be burdened again by a yoke of slavery" (Galatians 5:1, NIV).

It is, therefore, possible to be set free spiritually and not to be living in freedom in other parts of our lives. This is not the fullness of what Christ died for. At the moment we become Christians, God begins transforming us to set us free from bondage and draw us closer to Him. Even though I knew I was set free, in hiddenness, I realized that I wasn't walking fully free. I had issues and mindsets that were holding me a slave to fear. I found I didn't fully trust in God's timing and sovereignty over my life, and so if circumstances didn't unfold like I thought they should, then I was left frustrated and disappointed. Learning to fully trust God with all my heart and find my hope in Him enabled me to find peace with whatever circumstance God led me into. Striving ceased, and I was able to live in the present moment more easily. My fifteen-year plan for my life now became another tool to help guide me, but I wasn't a slave to it anymore or in fear that I had missed out. God's grace really is sufficient to live fully in the moment.

Make no mistake; God is fully committed to this process of setting us free and bringing about deep transformation in our lives, especially in the hidden seasons. The question is, are you?

Self Reflection

- How fully are you embracing this "hidden" season? What does that look like?

- In what areas of your life do you recognize "the old man" dying?

- What areas of your life are you resisting the transformational work of God? *Take time to ask Holy Spirit to reveal the answer to this question and the reasons for why you might be doing so.*

- Do you feel in any rush to see transformation happen in your life?

- What can you learn from the caterpillar's journey to transformation?

Chapter 8: To Be Embraced

To embrace something is to welcome it with open arms and to accept it completely. This is the challenge of the hidden season, knowing that it can be painful when our identity is confronted.

> In each season of hiddenness, our sense of value is disrupted. Stripped of what others affirmed us to be, we are left staring at our undecorated selves, wondering what makes us truly special ... In this season God intends to give us an unshakable identity in Him that no amount of adoration nor rejection can alter.
>
> ***Anonymous: Jesus' Hidden Years...and Yours***
>
> **(page 115) Alicia Britt Cole**

This is the identity of the trees spoken about in Jeremiah 17:8 that are planted along the riverbank with deep roots stretching into the water. They are neither bothered by the heat nor long months of drought, and their leaves are always green and their fruit continual. They are unshakable and thrive whatever the season. God has designed each one of us to be like these trees by the river of His love, thriving in all seasons of life. My question to you is...do you believe it?

We will face painful times and challenging circumstances where we feel concealed from the world around us and where waiting is our portion. Times where our deepest longings seem far from our grasp or something of the past. Times where applause is silent and affirmation runs thin. However, in these seasons, God does not want us to be rocked in our identity. He is committed to exposing areas where we desperately need more of Him. He joins us in the center of our pain only to knit us more intimately with Himself as we acknowledge the true source of our hope, our longing, and our dreams. The hidden seasons are a key component of our growth that God Himself draws us into because He loves us.

Apostle Paul spent fourteen years hidden. After a spectacular conversion, he moves to Tarsus, where there is almost no record of any public ministry. Many scholars call this "the lost years" due to the scarcity of any recorded activity compared to all other stages of his ministry. I would suggest that these were the "hidden years" where God began shaping in him an unshakable identity that learned the art of contentment in all situations. Paul wrote this later in his life:

> I know how to get along with humble means, and I also know how to live in prosperity; in any and every circumstance I have learned the secret of being filled and going hungry, both of having abundance and suffering need.
>
> **Philippians 4:12 (NASB)**

Paul learned to thrive in all seasons. He knew what it meant to live in the ebb and flow of life, seasons of abundance, as well as the more challenging ones. In fact, he had come to a place where he embraced trials knowing that God's transformational work is bringing about the very thing that we all desperately need in order to stay the course and not give up...hope.

Look what Paul says about it:

> And not only this, but we also exult in our tribulations, knowing that tribulation brings about perseverance; and perseverance, proven character; and proven character, hope; and hope does not disappoint, because the love of God has been poured out within our hearts through the Holy Spirit who was given to us.
>
> **Romans 5:3–5 (NASB)**

When we find hope in God through the painful times of waiting and being hidden, there is a promise that we will not be disappointed. Why is that?

Well, as Paul embraces what God is doing and surrenders to God's timing, he finds a depth of satisfaction in his relationship with God that is greater than any fulfilled dream. Now he is able to claim that he is satisfied in all circumstances, all seasons of life. This is the true hope that

Paul found, an unshakable identity in Christ that neither affirmation or rejection nor hiddenness or spotlight could destroy. This is what we all need!

What we see happen in Paul's life during his public ministry tells us a lot about what he allowed God to shape in him through the fourteen years we don't see. God had become his anchor so that, in all circumstances, he learned to find peace and contentment through his intimate relationship with God.

Even the abusive years that Joseph faced when he was betrayed, forgotten, and held captive were not wasted or insignificant. God was not the author of the evil that came in Joseph's direction, but He was certainly the author of the faith and hope that was built in these circumstances. Joseph knew what it meant to wait for release and justice as an innocent man. Through this, he discovered his own personal relationship with the God of his forefathers in this place of obscurity and, in turn, discovered his true self. God used this time to shape him into a man who could rule a nation in a great time of need, not in arrogance but in humility, not in strength but in weakness, not by dominion but with a servant's heart.

It was the same with Jesus; the thirty hidden years were an ordained part of His journey on Earth. These years were not in the public eye, doing what we read about in the Gospels, but they were just as significant and necessary as the time He spent discipling His followers and publicly displaying the kingdom of God with signs and wonders. Anonymous, Jesus grew in favor with God and man as He learned to hear the voice of His heavenly Father, receive unconditional love, and submit to the Father's leading and timing. This love shaped who He was, and, in turn, He was able to reflect the Father's heart to the broken world around Him with deep compassion yet unshaken by public opinion. Jesus knew what it meant to be a beloved Son of God and enjoy His pleasure throughout His life, no matter the circumstance. Imagine if Jesus had not submitted to the Father's timing, whose kingdom would He be building? God's, His own, or Satan's?

I don't believe that Jesus was in any rush to start a public ministry, even though He would have been burdened with the Father's love for the world and wanting to accurately portray that. His thirty years of anonymity were lived to the full, living out His role as a son to Mary and Joseph, a brother, and a friend, doing the ordinary things that those around Him did. He trusted the Father's timing for Him and lived peacefully in that knowledge every day of His life. Jesus lived life abundantly whether He was hidden or in the public eye, whether concealed or released!

The years of being anonymous, unrevealed, and unrecognized were precious, purposeful years that Jesus and many others in the Bible fully embraced. It's now our turn to embrace this season as believers, recognizing its purpose of bringing about transformation within us.

Everyone, at some point in their life, is faced with hiddenness to some degree. In hidden times, we are faced with the depths of our relational identity, learning to live freely as a child of God in difficult circumstances and the challenge of waiting for God's timing. These things can only be learned in challenging times where the heat is turned up and what we really believe is exposed. Without this season, we run the risk of being a slave to the adoration or rejection of man and, at best, a fair-weather Christian.

I have also come to discover the beauty of hiddenness as God has drawn me deeper and deeper into Him and affirmed me as His daughter in Christ. I am no longer driven to bring about my destiny but feel the freedom to be led by the Holy Spirit on the journey, more at peace with God's timing.

Remember my definition of hiddenness that I shared early on:

The difference between who I know I am called to be and what I am called to do versus my current reality. I have come to see this through a different lens, one that has purpose and meaning in the tension of the "not yet." I am more able to recognize the significance of every day, whether in anonymity or on the public stage, and know that grace abounds daily to help me live freely in Jesus. Some days, this has its challenges, especially when the yearning for what God has placed within me cries out to see more. However, it is much easier to find peace in these times as my roots are deeper and more secure in God than they used to be. My relational identity is getting harder to shake now!

Whenever the fears arise that I have missed it or that it's too late to see the things fulfilled that God has revealed to me, I consider Jesus. I ponder what He may have been feeling at twenty-eight years old, how "He offered up both prayers and pleas with loud crying and tears" (Hebrews 5:7, NASB), and yet His yearning was pure and unselfishly motivated. I think about His longing to see His Father glorified, God's chosen people set free, the destruction of the enemy's work, and the goodness of God revealed through signs and wonders. I consider Jesus as He chose to wait on the Father's timing and submit to the Father's plan. Jesus knew His cries did not fall on deaf ears; He was secure in the fact that "he was heard because of his reverend submission" (Hebrews 5:7, NIV). Jesus had a hope in God that He knew would not disappoint. As I consider Jesus and how He positioned His heart in the veiled place, I am once again encouraged, hope rises up, and

I feel an invitation from God to go deeper. An invitation to embrace the now just as it is.

Fellow believers, this is exactly what this season is; an invitation. God Himself is inviting us into a deeper, more fruitful relationship with Him that anchors our identity and draws us into living in the present moment. This is how we thrive!

Choosing to wait on God's timing in hiddenness is an invitation from God to position our hearts in an active state of expectancy. It's a time to become rooted in the things above:

> Since, then, you have been raised with Christ, set your hearts on things above, where Christ is, seated at the right hand of God. Set your minds on things above, and not on earthly things. For you died, and your life is now hidden with Christ in God.

Colossians 3:1–3 (NIV)

A life hidden with Christ in God is dead to the worldly things that so easily entangle and snare us from growing deeper with God, ourselves, and others. Some of that includes our false expectations of how the promises of God should come about or when we think we should see things happen. It's about letting go of our rights to be blessed and successful in the eyes of those around us. We have been raised with Christ and so are empowered to set our hearts on things above. Everything that is above is life-giving and leads us to more freedom.

God is committed to exposing our false expectations, which hold us captive, and by doing so, He redirects our hope to the Lord, and we are drawn into deeper intimacy with Him. God draws us into an active state of expectancy, keeping us present and aware of what God is doing in the "now," and hope reigns in this place no matter what the circumstance.

It's time for us to embrace this season of our lives when we know that it's God's hand that conceals us in this place. Even though we may feel ready to be released, geared up for prophetic words to come about, and desperate to see prayers answered, we need to find peace with the reality that God's timing runs on a different clock. We have seen how the Bible is full of people who found purpose and meaning in hiddenness and how God was all the time active on their behalf, shaping the person, arranging the pieces, and establishing the firm foundations for the future.

Hiddenness is not meaningless and stagnant but significant and active. My prayer is that you would embrace this season, knowing that God has designed you to walk through this and thrive in it just like Jesus. As you do so, you will find that

God is right in the midst of it with you, waiting to reveal to you who you really are and, better still, to unveil Himself.

Self Reflection

- Does your sense of value change when you are affirmed or rejected by others?

- From 0–10, how unshakeable is your identity in Christ?

- What does it mean to you to set your mind on things above and not on earthly things? How can this help you find peace with God's timing?

- What are two things that God is doing in you in this season that you can embrace and take more of an active part in? e.g., For me, I recognized that God was encouraging me to live more in the present moment and not be so focused on the future and fulfillment of dreams. So, I began to spend time in the morning thanking God for what was currently happening in my life, even the trials I was facing, and then praying for the day ahead. I also focused my journaling on what was going on around me and what God had done that day rather than daydreaming about the future.

References

Cole, Alicia Britt. *Anonymous: Jesus' Hidden Years...and Yours.* Integrity Publishers, 2006.

Brower, Lincoln. "Inside the Chrysalis." Journey North: Monarch butterfly, n.d. https://journeynorth.org/tm/monarch/ChrysalisDevelopmentLPB.html.

CPSIA information can be obtained
at www.ICGtesting.com
Printed in the USA
BVHW051534020123
655384BV00026B/335